THIS

WALK

WAY

WALK THIS WAY

INCARNATIONAL DISCIPLESHIP
GROWING FAITH SERIES

ACE MCCLINTON

THIS WALK WAY

An eight-week course designed to train and equip God's people for works of good service through a highly effective disciple-making strategy that embraces incarnational discipleship. This book will be quick to read, but difficult to practice.

Copyright © 2014 by Ace McClinton. All rights reserved.

WALK THIS WAY
Published by Aleletos Publishing Media, LLC.
801 Longwood Drive
Joliet, Illinois 60432 U.S.A.

Printed in the United States of America   ISBN-13 978-0-615-99394-2

Except for brief excerpts for review purposes, no part of this publication may be reproduced, stored in a retrieval system, or transmitted in any form or by any means, electronic, mechanical, photocopying, recording, scanning, or otherwise permitted under Section 107 or 108 of the 1976 United States Copyright Act, without either the prior written permission of the publisher, or authorization through payment of the appropriate per-copy fee to the Copyright Clearance Center, Inc., 222 Rosewood Drive, Danvers, MA 01923, 978-750-8400, fax 978-646-8600, or on the Web at www.copyright.com.

Limit of Liability/Disclaimer of Warranty: While the publisher and author have used their best efforts in preparing this book, they make no representation or warranties with respect to the accuracy or completeness of the contents of this book and specifically disclaim any implied warranties of merchantability or fitness for a particular purpose. No warranty may be created or extended by sales representatives or written sales material. The advice and strategies contained herein may not be suitable for your situation. You should consult with a professional where appropriate. Neither the publisher nor author shall be liable for any loss of profit or any other commercial damages, including but not limited to special, incidental, consequential, or other damages.

Aleletos Publishing also publishes its books in a variety of electronic formats. Some content that appears in print may not be available in electronic form as well as some electronic content may not be available in print form.

Unless otherwise noted the majority of Scripture is taken from the HOLY BIBLE, NEW INTERNATIONAL VERSION®. NIV®. Copyright © 1973, 1978, 1984 by International Bible Society. Used by permission of Zondervan. All rights reserved.

Scripture taken from The HOLY BIBLE, ENGLISH STANDARD VERSION Copyright © 2001 by Crossway Bibles, a division of Good News Publishers. All rights reserved.

Scripture taken from THE MESSAGE. Copyright© 1993, 1994, 1995, 1996, 2000, 2001, 2002. Used by permission of NavPress Publishing Group.

Scripture taken from THE AMPLIFIED BIBLE, EXPANDED EDITION. Copyright© 1987 by the Zondervan Corporation and The Lockman Foundation. All rights reserved. The Amplified Bible® , copyright © 1965, 1987. The Amplified Old Testament, Part One, copyright © 1964; The Amplified Old Testament, Part Two, copyright © 1962 by the Zondervan Corporation. The Amplified New Testament, copyright © 1958, 1987; The Amplified Gospel of John, copyright © 1954, 1987 by The Lockman Foundation, La Habra, CA 90631.

Scripture taken from HOLY BIBLE. NEW LIVING TRANSLATION. Copyright© 1996, 2004, 2007 by Tyndale House Foundation. Used by permission of Tyndale House Publishers Inc., Carol Stream, Illinois 60188. All rights reserved.

A significant portion of the proceeds from the sale of all Aleletos Publishing books go to help spread the gospel of Christ to all nations in our generation!

The vision of Aleletos Publishing is to use biblical teaching to advance the gospel of Christ and bring glory to God.

To my wife,
Pamela
and children,
Enders, Masai, Somiya and Declan.
Thank you all for your help,
quiet and coffee runs.

CONTENTS

Acknowledgements	xi
Introduction	xii
Part One: THE CALL TO DISCIPLESHIP	15
Day 1: Follow Me	19
Day 2: Let Your Light Shine	23
Day 3: The Kingdom or Bust	29
Day 4: The Short Answer…Pray	33
Day 5: The Rock	41
Day 6: Don't Test Me!	45
Day 7: We Worship Him	49
Day 8: Anger Management	53
Day 9: Living By Truth	57
Day 10: Top Ten	63
Part Two: GROWING IN THE GRACE	66
Day 11: Know Mercy	69
Day 12: The Extra Mile	77
Day 13: The Way	83
Day 14: The Harvest is Plentiful	87
Day 15: Freely Give	91
Day 16: Heal the Sick	95
Day 17: The Untouchables	103
Day 18: Raise the Dead	107
Day 19: Drive out Demons	111
Day 20: Shrewd Yet Innocent	115

Part Three: DANGEROUS AND UNLAWFUL   121

Day 21: Have No Fear   123

Day 22: Some Things are Certain   127

Day 23: Unashamed   131

Day 24: New Wine Skins   135

Day 25: Watch Out!   139

Day 26: Love, Trust and Obey   143

Day 27: Keep Watch   147

Day 28: Lay Down Your Burdens   151

Day 29: Careless Words   155

Day 30: Guard Against Hypocrisy   159

Part Four: GREATER HUMILITY   163

Day 31: Praise Make Stupid   165

Day 32: A Fool is Always Right   169

Day 33: The Greatest in the Kingdom   173

Day 34: Love One Another Like Jesus   177

Day 35: The Agony of the Feet   181

Day 36: Help for the Hurt   185

Day 37: Plank vs. Speck   191

Day 38: Be a Well of Forgiveness   195

Day 39: Remain in Me   199

Day 40: Do This   203

Day 41: Go Make Disciples   209

Acknowledgements

"All hard work brings a profit, but mere talk leads to poverty," according to Proverbs 14:23. When I think of this passage I think of no other person than my wife and all the hard work she has done over the years we have been married. My wife is the hardest working person I know and without her help this work and others like it would not have been possible. I would like to thank her for her encouragement, her diligence in educating and training our children and her unwavering love for me and our dreams. I could hardly imagine God sending me a more suitable partner in the gospel.

Introduction

"If anyone chooses to do God's will, he will find out whether my teaching comes from God or whether I speak on my own." – John 7:17

in· car· na· tion· al [in-kahr-ney-sh*uh*-nl]

a person embodying or exhibiting a quality, idea, or the nature and character of someone.

dis· ci· ple· ship [dih-sahy-puh l-ship]

the process of being transformed into the likeness of Jesus Christ.

Incarnational discipleship is the principle by which the teachings of Jesus are modeled in the lives of people and taught through a call to imitate these godly characteristics in a purposeful relationship. Often we focus more on learning than doing and we end with being educated beyond our obedience. Jesus taught by modeling an example he wanted his disciples to follow. Education should consist of both learning and doing.

Through the Great Commission we understand that Jesus commands us to teach these newly baptized disciples to obey everything he commanded us. In an effort to equip others and reproduce these training principles so that workers are effectively multiplied. At this level of leadership we already possess the curriculum to educate – we need only apply it. Whether you are new to the faith or you are several years in the faith, this book is designed to help you learn and teach the principles Jesus taught in his ministry.

In this Growing Faith series, we will learn from Jesus to obey his commands and follow closely in his footsteps. This study is designed to be used in conjunction with the person who will be mentoring you in the faith as they will be training you in these principles. Typically this person is whoever has been actively involved in your relationship with God. You may have studied the Bible together, explored deep matters of your belief system or they were simply a friend from work who invited you to church. The Hebrew writer (which is most likely Paul) conveys this same notion by saying, "Remember your leaders, who spoke the word of God to you. Consider the outcome of their way of life and imitate their faith." (Hebrews 13:7 NIV). In which case you are either a person who has decided to take a greater role in someone's life by becoming a spiritual leader to someone or this book was suggested to you by your discipleship mentor ("discipler").

A discipleship mentor faithfully desires to hold to the teachings of Jesus by being a person worthy of imitation. The apostle Paul demonstrated this same heart in his letter to the church in Corinth, "Follow my example, as I follow the example of Christ" (1 Corinthians 11:1 NIV).

"Therefore I urge you to imitate me. For this reason I have sent to you Timothy, my son whom I love, who is faithful in the Lord. He will remind you of my way of life in Christ Jesus, which agrees with what I teach everywhere in every church." – 1 Corinthians 4:16, 17 (NIV)

"On the contrary, we worked night and day, laboring and toiling so that we would not be a burden to any of you. We did this, not because we do not have the right to such help, but in order to offer ourselves as a model for you to imitate." – 2 Thessalonians 3:8 (NIV).

All these passages teach a principle that was practiced throughout the first-century by disciples who walked with Jesus and those they taught who in turn taught others. "And the things you have heard me say in the presence of many witnesses entrust to reliable people who will also be qualified to teach others" (2 Timothy 2:2 NIV).

This person who has demonstrated to be reliable with the word of God will partner with you in this guide as you live out these daily challenges. It will help if you do not look at your discipler as simply your mentor in the faith, but as you would see Jesus – after all we are called to make disciples of Jesus (not of ourselves).

The goal for this series is to get you to see Jesus and learn from him. In order to accomplish this you will have to look past the flesh and fix your eyes on Jesus, the author and perfecter of your faith (Hebrews 12:2).

"Whoever has my commands and obeys them, he is the one who loves me." – John 14:21

Part One: THE CALL TO DISCIPLESHIP

For a moment I want you to close your eyes and imagine Jesus is reclining on a grassy patch at the top of a mountainous plain. The stars are out and you are gathered with other disciples around a fire as Jesus begins to teach. You are a little nervous to have been selected by Jesus to follow him because there was nothing special about you to have been chosen. You have never had a sophisticated background in religious education and you did not fit the stereotypical pattern of someone who should be considered for such a task. Jesus begins by saying, *"Each day you will be given an activity that will help you put my words into practice in order to obey all I command. You will be walking with me each day on this journey. You will rise early with me as I wake up to give glory to God the Father. You will follow me as I go out to seek and to save that which was lost. You will learn how to love your brothers and sisters as I love you. And at the end of your training, you will go out and do this for others as I have been doing with you."*

Your heart races and you smile as you unconsciously nod toward Jesus with an affirming, "Yes!" Jesus looks back at you with an expression that communicates to you, "You are ready to begin."

WEEK ONE

"You diligently study the Scriptures because you think that by them you possess eternal life. These are the Scriptures that testify about me, yet you refuse to come to me to have life." – John 5:39, 40.

FOLLOW ME

Day 1: Follow Me

Before Jesus began his ministry on earth, many religious leaders taught their disciples in a classroom and expected them to memorize and regurgitate. Jesus directly confronts this in the character of the Pharisees. Jesus knows that salvation cannot be found in memorizing books of the Bible or intensive study of language and text.

Jesus wants us to follow him.

"If anyone is thirsty, let him come to me and drink." – John 7:37

Jesus' way of teaching was radically different and did not require the extensive and exhaustive formula of the Pharisees or traditional teaching. Jesus' teaching was not in the form of taking tests or long lectures. Jesus taught in every situation and called his disciples to take note of what He did.

We follow a similar pattern in many activities we attempt in life. If a person desires to learn the skill of fixing cars, she will learn from a skilled mechanic who can show her exactly what she needs to know to be successful at her craft. This is not to say we should eliminate the educational component from training, but there is an obvious advantage to an apprentice model of learning than simply learning in a classroom setting.

This limitation in the educational system has been noted by a frustrated educator who denotes a needed improvement in the way teaching can be modified to incorporate more "doing." Dr. Mitchell believes "observing" is more than simply listening or seeing passively but actively practicing what is being taught.[1]

In 2007 my wife and I decided to pack up the family and move to Los Angeles California to go and train for ministry. Sure we could have read more books about evangelism, but I wanted to learn from others who were being effective in their faith with evangelizing their cities.

---

[1] Dr. Michael Mitchell, *Leading, Teaching, and Making Disciples* (Bloomington, IN: CrossBooks, 2010), 204, 307.

I knew from my financial education that I needed someone who was financially successful to help me get "over the fence." I had formed poor spending, saving and investing habits for too long to attempt such a feat alone. Similarly, many of us find a coach or a boot-camp if we are serious about slimming down and toning up. We need a spiritual coach and Jesus is our ultimate life coach.

"Come, follow me, 'Jesus said,' and I will make you fishers of men." – Mark 1:17.

Imitate Christ. Be a fisher of men as an overall pattern of living.

Reflection and Practical Application

1. Pray early in the morning and start your day as Jesus did by getting outside to a solitary place.
2. Learn from your situation as you allow yourself to be challenged by meeting someone new today.
3. Make yourself available to your discipling partner and see what he or she has in store for you today.

"You are the light of the world. A city on a hill cannot be hidden. Neither do people light a lamp and put it under a bowl. Instead they put it on its stand, and it gives light to everyone in the house. In the same way, let your light shine before men, that they may see your good deeds and praise your Father in heaven." **– Matthew 5:14-17**

LET YOUR LIGHT SHINE

Day 2: Let Your Light Shine

Some say the greatest difference between disciples justified freely by the grace of God and a "good person" is the consistency in which each person lives. A disciple does "good" and works to please God in heaven by his deeds and may on occasion do "bad." A "good person" lives to please himself and on occasion may do "good."

"The body of Christ is like a city within a city," was once said very eloquently and no city that is placed on a hill can be hidden. Many churches have grown to the size of some small towns and the powerful effect we can have on the cities we live in can be measured by the praise we bring to God.

Many times we think of lofty acts to do in order to accomplish this command of Jesus. However, it is often the small things that are the most welcomed and illicit great praise to God.

Imagine the middle of Spring when winter has officially ended and the weather has warmed to cool light jacket temperatures. Normally, in the North the weather during this time is often in the mild 70s. However, this day was record-breaking heat and for this time of year anything over 80 degrees will be unexpected, difficult to plan around, and just as fascinating as snow in Southern Mississippi. This was the condition of my sister's graduation.

The heat of the day quickly poured into the poorly ventilated auditorium. Large industrial fans only seemed to circulate the heat around the room. Graduates waited patiently in their assigned seats near the front of the stage until each speaker made their way to the podium. Unable to move during the commencement, these tormented Graduates remained seated attempting to fan the poorly circulated hot air through their heavy robes with their caps. The guests, however, were afforded some relief with water in cooler dispensers in the back – far out of reach for the graduating students.

There was one disciple who brought a relative water as the disciple's relative was in the graduating party. After seeing the other graduates' reactions to the relief, this disciple had compassion on the crowd and began to bring water two cups at a time to the remaining graduates. Because the kingdom belongs to such as these, there were children who began to help by bringing cups of water and made the work even more enjoyable as spectators began to be amused by their efforts.

At the end of the ceremony the graduates mentioned to one another (not to the disciple) that this person was their savior. Though, "Thank God" may have been said in cliché, there is no doubt that good deeds such as these bring praise to our Father in heaven.

I can also remember on another occasion when three of my closest friends and I sat and talked about a movie we saw and were discussing the spiritual implications of the film at a restaurant. We enjoyed each other's favor and spoke joyfully and freely about new discoveries we were learning in our faith. As we laughed and continued to talk more, two young women came over to our table and asked us where we go to church. We were pleasantly surprised that we heard such an unsolicited response simply because we were excited about being in each other's company.

Letting our lights shine involves doing such good deeds that it causes others to question what makes us different. Being a light in a dark city is also showing people the love we have living in us. These two young women were amazed by what they saw and wanted to know what was at the source of our joy.

When we live our lives like lights in the world we create opportunities for God's glory to shine in the lives of others. Jesus' life was full of joy in the Holy Spirit and he was the most joyful person wherever he went. People were drawn to Jesus and wanted to be around him – all the time. Why else would Jesus force people to go home after being together for nearly three days (Mark 8:9)? We lose all track of time when we are excited about the people we are around.

Reflection and Practical Application

1. For today ... let your light shine. Let others see the vibrant and joyful relationships you have in Christ.
2. This week, joyfully give to someone unexpectedly and look for opportunities to brighten up the day of someone else.

"Therefore I tell you, **do not worry about your life**, what you will eat or drink; or about your body, what you will wear. Is not life more important than food, and the body more important than clothes? Look at the birds of the air; they do not sow or reap or store away in barns, and yet your heavenly Father feeds them. Are you not much more valuable than they? Who of you by worrying can add a single hour to his life?

And why do you worry about clothes? See how the lilies of the field grow. They do not labor or spin. Yet I tell you that not even Solomon in all his splendor was dressed like one of these. If that is how God clothes the grass of the field, which is here today and tomorrow is thrown into the fire, will he not much more clothe you, O you of little faith? So **do not worry**, saying, 'What shall we eat?' or 'What shall we drink?' or 'What shall we wear?' For the pagans run after all these things, and your heavenly Father knows that you need them. But **seek first his kingdom and his righteousness**, and all these things will be given to you as well. Therefore **do not worry about tomorrow**, for tomorrow will worry about itself. Each day has enough trouble of its own." – **Matthew 6:25-34**

THE KINGDOM OR BUST

Day 3: The Kingdom or Bust

Why is seeking first the kingdom of God so significant? When we understand the significance of the kingdom in the gospel message, then we understand the importance of entering it as well. Jesus commands us to preach the message of the kingdom, "As you go, preach this message: 'The kingdom of heaven is near.'" – Matthew 10:7. Also in Matthew 4:23, "Jesus went throughout Galilee, teaching in their synagogues, preaching the good news of the kingdom, and healing every disease and sickness among the people," **we see the message of the kingdom is the good news. Why is this news so good? Because being in the**

kingdom literally means salvation. To enter the kingdom means resting in the assurance of salvation at the point of entry rather than a common perception of St. Peter giving a "go/no go" pass to enter the "pearly gates." Jesus said the kingdom **_of_** heaven and not heaven itself (though the two are not disconnected). In fact, looking more closely at the Daniel prophecy we see God's intent was to expand his kingdom in heaven to earth first through Jesus (the Rock) by crushing all the other kingdoms. Even Scripture says our spirit rests in heaven with Jesus (Ephesians 2:6). Oddly, we exist both here on earth and heaven – a dual citizenship (Philippians 3:20).

Jesus commands us not to worry. Paul, as a disciple of Jesus, confirms this in Philippians 4:6. Even the good doctor Luke as a third generation disciple (Paul's ministry) carries on Jesus' commands including this one in Luke 12:22.

Life is full of worries and concern. We worry about our family. We worry about our children. We worry about our jobs and retirement. We worry about our health. We worry about tomorrow. We worry about next week. We worry about last week. We worry about next year. We worry about the next ten years. We worry, we worry, we worry. The irony is that none of our worrying accomplishes much of anything, other than possibly reducing our life expectancy and creating unwanted health concerns. Studies have shown that this type of negative stress can cause many negative health conditions.[2]

---

[2] Richard A. Swenson, *Margin: Restoring Emotional, Physical, Financial, and Time Reserves to Overloaded Lives* (Colorado Springs: NavPress, 2004), 47.

Jesus gives us the solution in a simple command. If we put the kingdom first before our careers or homes or other worries and place them in the hands of Him who can actually help, then we become like children who trust their parents to take care of their every need. God is our Father who knows what we need and eagerly desires to lavish his love on us.

Giving up all we have can be challenging and we are often faced with this decision many times. However, because we made this decision as disciples, we can be sure that we have the seeds of this faith for when the times come to rise to these challenges again.

Reflection and Practical Application

1. Think of three major areas of concern in your life.
2. Share these areas with your discipler.
3. Decide to put the kingdom first in all you do.

"And when you pray, do not be like the hypocrites, for they love to pray standing in the synagogues and on the street corners to be seen by men. I tell you the truth, they have received their reward in full. But when you pray, go into your room, close the door and pray to your Father, who is unseen. Then your Father, who sees what is done in secret, will reward you. And when you pray, do not keep on babbling like pagans, for they think they will be heard because of their many words. Do not be like them, for your Father knows what you need before you ask him." –
Matthew 6:5-15

THE SHORT ANSWER...
PRAY

Day 4: The Short Answer...Pray

Jesus takes away our religious crutches. Whether it is giving to charity and announcing it with trumpets or praying to be seen by others. Jesus calls us to worship God in spirit and in truth.

Ironically, many people do not believe the sin of the Pharisees apply to Christians today. However, we see sin is common to man and can easily entangle. Our prayers can become imitations of lofty prayers. We can use repetition to replace thoughtful moments. Jesus commands us not to be like this. In other words, Jesus desires our prayers to be sincere and true. Jesus is telling us not to be like hypocrites who only pretend to be praying. What is pretend prayer?

Prayer without faith is pretend prayer. Prayer that is for the benefit of being seen as spiritual is pretend prayer. After telling us how not to pray Jesus again does not give a lecture or a quiz. He simply demonstrates and gives us an outline.

One of the most simple and humble prayers in Scripture is found in Genesis 24, "Then he prayed, "Lord, God of my master Abraham, make me successful today, and show kindness to my master Abraham. See, I am standing beside this spring, and the daughters of the townspeople are coming out to draw water. May it be that when I say to a young woman, 'Please let down your jar that I may have a drink,' and she says, 'Drink, and I'll water your camels too'—let her be the one you have chosen for your servant Isaac. By this I will know that you have shown kindness to my master." Before he had finished praying, Rebekah came out with her jar on her shoulder." – Genesis 24:12-15 (NIV).

This humble servant of Abraham prayed with faith, earnestness and an eagerness to see God accomplish his request. In addition to that his prayer was specific. Often our prayers can be vague and too general to see the power of God move in our lives. Abraham's servant asked God to show him the right woman by completing a very specific task. Even more remarkable than his faith is the speed with which God answered his prayer. While he was still praying, Scripture records Rebekah coming out with her jar ready to either be the woman literally of his prayers or the first of many he would reject until God revealed the correct future wife for Isaac.

Why do our fifteen minute, thirty-minute or even hour long prayers lack the type of faith-moving results of this 23 word, thirty-second prayer by a Gentile? It is no wonder why Jesus often used Gentile and Samaritans as examples of great faith. Could it be that they lack the religious baggage that the Jewish people or "church-goers" have? Their examples of faith are simple and their examples of prayer are earnest. They truly desire Jesus to act on their behalf and they truly believe God will bring about what he promised.

Most often when I read books on prayer it will typically address the time spent in prayer. Most of us fall into this category because we all recognize how often we fall short in praying. In the morning somehow our day gets going without us and we find ourselves playing catch-up all day. We miss moments of prayer in the morning and we do not have enough time to dedicate to devoted prayer. We will still pray over meals and possibly before we get on the road to commute into work so that God will watch over our safety. However, we find ourselves missing a consistent morning routine that involves uninterrupted prayer to God.

So what do we do when we read books on prayer? We try to pray harder. By harder I mean we try harder to pray longer. We find ourselves lacking enough words to extend to a half-hour, let alone a full-hour. We can scarcely imagine getting close to the "super-spiritual" who can spend a whopping three hours in prayer. What are these prayer-warriors praying about anyways? Despite all this pressure to pray longer, I find it comforting to find passages in the

Bible that simply says, "be faithful in prayer" (Romans 12:12). It would seem based on Jesus' comparison of the prayer of the self-justifying Pharisees that our prayers should be full of faith rather than length. Many of my most powerful prayers were short and to the point. And wouldn't you know it, God answered those prayers quickly. My cowardly prayers may be long and give me a great sense of spirituality, but they are general and I never truly expect God to answer them – these are my "your will be done prayers." Not to be confused with a true desire of God's will to be done on earth as it is in heaven, but a faithless compromise that lets my faith off the hook if I don't see the result I requested. I'd rather see the power of God through short genuine prayers, than long faithless praying.

All throughout the gospels we see the power Jesus received through prayer. The evidence of this is revealed by his disciples asking him to teach them how to pray. We know the power of prayer even when it comes to spreading the gospel. That is, there are only certain demons that will come out through prayer and fasting – prayer being at the cornerstone.

When you pray say…

One of our biggest weaknesses in prayer as Christians is not knowing what to pray about. We can find ourselves praying without faith and power when we lack the words. Jesus' first lesson in prayer was to give his disciples instructions on what they should say. We use Jesus' words as an outline because there are other examples in Scripture that are not the word for word prayer found in Luke 11.

Communicate not Regurgitate

There are other outlines that can be used in praying. The A.C.T.S prayer outlines four sections of what to pray about. First A – adoration; then C – confession; next T – thanksgiving, and finally S – supplication. This outline is very similar to the one Jesus gives, but adds a few places to pray intercessory prayer, confession and thanksgiving. These instructions on prayer are given in other places in Scripture.

Pray in the Name of Jesus *(John 16:23-24)*

Imagine you need an important request approved by your mayor. You draft a proposal and letter and as you're ready to send it you get a call from the President of the United States giving you permission to attach his name as the author of the document. How has your confidence changed as to the approval of your request? This is in effect the authority Jesus has given us to use his name in prayer. We are sending our requests to God with Jesus' seal of approval stamped right below. An even more accurate example would be if the President's only son or daughter signed in crayon their name at the bottom of our requests. Jesus always did what pleased God and because of Jesus' reverent submission he was always heard by God. This is what Jesus is giving us by commanding us to pray in his name.

Reflection and Practical Application

1. Learning the importance of prayer is paramount and will set a foundation for your prayer life going forward.

2. Find an example of someone who will pray with you out loud and with fervor.
3. Practice Jesus' commands by:
    a. Praying in secret (Matthew 6:5)
    b. Pray briefly, but with power (don't babble)
    c. Pray throughout the day, be persistent (Luke 18:1-7)
    d. Be specific with your requests (Matthew 7:7-11)
    e. Be faithful in prayer, believe you have received (Mark 11:22)
    f. Choose a day to fast in secret with a difficult prayer (Matthew 6:16-18).

"Therefore everyone who hears these words of mine and puts them into practice is like a wise man who built his house on the rock. The rain came down, the streams rose, and the winds blew and beat against that house; yet it did not fall, because it had its foundation on the rock. But everyone who hears these words of mine and does not put them into practice is like a foolish man who built his house on sand. The rain came down, the streams rose, and the winds blew and beat against that house, and it fell with a great crash."

– Matthew 7:24-27

THE ROCK

Day 5: The Rock

God is not judging us based on how much information we can retain and regurgitate concerning the Scriptures. We will not have a test on the books of the Bible or who's who in the Bible. Many people can quote from the Bible, but not many are putting the words of the Bible into practice consistently. *It is the doing, not the telling that reveals the foundation of the house.*

Put My Words Into Practice

Every day I wake up and read how many sit ups I should do to gain the highly advertised promise of "steel abs." However, I never actually do any sit ups, or leg lifts, or stomach crunches. It is the same way with our faith. If we consistently put Jesus' words into practice we will start to see the faith building results of these actions. Likewise, if we only read the words, but do not put them into practice, we are the same as the person who hopes to get in shape but never does.

Not Just Bread Alone

"Jesus answered, "It is written: 'Man does not live on bread alone, but on every word that comes from the mouth of God.'" – Matthew 4:4

Why is this important? Satan uses partial truths and parts of Scripture to distort what is true to promote the lie. If we only focus on the New Testament alone or a few key passages we will miss the complete truth of the gospel. Focusing on a few passages have produced some of the most confusing and controversial teachings in all Christendom. Paul wrote through the Holy Spirit, "All Scripture is God-breathed."

All the Scriptures

"And beginning with Moses and all the Prophets, he explained to them what was said in all the Scriptures concerning himself." – Luke 24:27

"All Scripture is God-breathed and is useful for teaching, rebuking, correcting and training in righteousness, so that the man of God may be thoroughly equipped for every good work." – 2 Timothy 3:16, 17.

Paul received the gospel from Jesus through revelation and his message was confirmed by Peter, James and John. Paul's abridged writings do not contradict nor supersede Jesus' words. Luke (being in Paul's ministry) wrote and recorded Jesus' standard for becoming a follower of Jesus (Luke 9:23-26, Luke 14:25-33). Preaching a gospel that is devoid of Jesus' own words contained in the gospel writings should raise a red flag for anyone who seriously desires to pursue a path of discipleship.

Paul's writings would not therefore conflict with Luke's gospel as this would produce two teachings in contradiction and make Paul a poor teacher or Luke a poor student. Contradictions produce divisions and divisions threaten and tear at the fabric of unity within God's church. Without a deep and sincere love for the word of God that rises over and above our own selfish pursuits we can find ourselves as catalysts to the root of many divisions among professed Christians.

Reflection and Practical Application

1. Today, determine that you will get a plan to read and study the entire Bible.
2. Recall from Scripture one thing you know you are not putting into practice. Whether it is sharing your faith consistently, denying yourself daily, confessing sin regularly, praying on all occasions or giving generously. Determine what you know and what you are failing to put into practice.

"If you are the Son of God, " he said, "throw yourself down. For it is written:

"'He will command his angels concerning you,

and they will lift you up in their hands,

so that you will not strike your foot against a stone.'"

Jesus answered him, "It is also written: 'Do not put the Lord your God to the test." – Matthew 4:6, 7.

DON'T TEST ME

Day 6: Don't Test Me!

At some point in time we have either heard our parents say, have said, or have heard someone else's parent say, "Don't test me!" What does that person mean when they say that to their children? We know that if a child continues to press an issue or persist in a certain behavior after being warned by their parent, that ultimately punishment will ensue. The punishment may not happen after the first warning because the parent is being gracious or simply preoccupied with something else. However, when those infamous words, "Don't test me!" happen we know that the wrath of the parent is imminent.

Our heavenly Father disciplines us as our earthly fathers have done, but even to a greater degree with more patience and more love. When Jesus was tempted by Satan to prove he was the Son of God by diving off a cliff, **Jesus knew it was not right to test God** in this way. Would we pick up deadly snakes because it is written? Would we jump in front of a car or bus because it is written? What would these actions prove other than our own lack of faith?

Do Not Put God to Test

Much in the same way we sin without thought of repentance is how we test God in foolish actions. It is written that sin leads to death and to persist in sin is to test God.

The irony is that **Jesus proves he is the Son of God** in Luke 4 as he is rushed through a town by an angry mob in order to be thrown off a cliff. Jesus walks right through the crowd. No special guard or force was used. What changes an angry mob with blood lust to kill a man by throwing him down a cliff? Interesting to note, they did not take him outside to stone him (which would have been easier). They were so angry they continued in their rage in order to not only drive him out of the town but to make sure he died violently on his way out. This can only be the hand of God that intervened to fulfill Scripture.

The fact is **God fulfills his promises.** There is no "magic formula" or "spiritual ability" that will identify you as a disciple. We think if we pray loud enough or prophesy, sacrifice or babble that we will be shown to be disciples. However, Jesus calls us to believe. We believe and completely put our trust in when we put it all on the line for Jesus by giving it all up and following him. We show ourselves to be disciples by our love. Love is the only distinguishing mark that Jesus says identifies our discipleship to others. For love trusts, it hopes, and it obeys God. Love is also the sign to us even when our hearts have condemned us as faithless (1 John 3:20) – "for God is greater than our hearts."

Reflection and Practical Application

1. Pray to not be led into temptation.
2. Resolve to trust in the salvation plan of God.

"Again, the devil took him to a very high mountain and showed him all the kingdoms of the world and their splendor. "All this I will give you," he said, "if you will bow down and worship me."

Jesus said to him, "Away from me, Satan! For it is written: 'Worship the Lord your God, and serve him only.'" **– Matthew 4:8-10**

WE WORSHIP HIM

Day 7: We Worship Him

It is said that Satan wants to be like God. We know that Satan masquerades as an angel of light as well as those who minister for him. It makes sense that Satan would want us to worship him as we would God. Sadly, many people are worshiping Satan, thinking they are worshiping God. One key indicator of worshiping Satan is the worship of money and possessions. In Matthew 4 the devil is trying to offer Jesus possessions, power and authority. When the promise of prosperity is the central theme to a message, you can be certain Satan is crouching nearby ready to pull the listeners into his snare.

Worship and Serve God Alone

Jesus gives us a new direction and guide to worship. Our worship consists of God first (not ourselves and prosperity) and serving him, rather than being served. Satan's message consists of "What about me?" and "I want this! Give to me, give to me!"

God and Money

"Do not store up for yourselves treasures on earth, where moth and rust destroy, and where thieves break in and steal. But store up for yourselves treasures in heaven, where moth and rust do not destroy, and where thieves do not break in and steal. For where your treasure is, there your heart will be also.

"The eye is the lamp of the body. If your eyes are good, your whole body will be full of light. But if your eyes are bad, your whole body will be full of darkness. If then the light within you is darkness, how great is that darkness!

"No one can serve two masters. Either he will hate the one and love the other, or he will be devoted to the one and despise the other. You cannot serve both God and Money." **– Matthew 6:19-24.**

We are called to worship and serve God alone. When money becomes our focus along with gaining and possessing things then we are no longer serving God, but we are serving another master. The master who we obey is truly our master. Who do we truly obey when it comes to our finances? Are we subject to God's mission and work schedule or another's? Additionally, in our zeal to forsake serving money we must not forget to be stewards who are accountable to God and pay what we owe. Jesus commands us to give to Caesar what is Caesar's and to God what is God's (Matthew 22:21). Money can be useful and we can use it to advance the kingdom. In the same way Paul says, "food for the stomach and the stomach for food." We eat to live and not live to eat. We must have money obey us rather than become mastered by it. We use money to live and promote the kingdom and charity. We do not live for money or things.

Use Wealth/Talent to Win Friends

"I tell you, use worldly wealth to gain friends for yourselves, so that when it is gone, you will be welcomed into eternal dwellings."
– Luke 16:9

We have all been given a measure of talent and gifts from God. We are called to use these worldly talents (or wealth) to win people. Paul's ambition was to win as many as possible. What is possible for you? How much talent has God blessed you with to win souls?

Reflection and Practical Application

1. Figure out your strengths.
2. Start using your home, money and possessions to win people.
3. Practice hospitality.

WEEK TWO

"You have heard that it was said to the people long ago, 'Do not murder, and anyone who murders will be subject to judgment.' But I tell you that anyone who is angry with his brother will be subject to judgment. Again, anyone who says to his brother, 'Raca,' is answerable to the Sanhedrin. But anyone who says, 'You fool!' will be in danger of the fire of hell.

"Therefore, if you are offering your gift at the altar and there remember that your brother has something against you, leave your gift there in front of the altar. First go and be reconciled to your brother; then come and offer your gift.

"Settle matters quickly with your adversary who is taking you to court. Do it while you are still with him on the way, or he may hand you over to the judge, and the judge may hand you over to the officer, and you may be thrown into prison. I tell you the truth, you will not get out until you have paid the last penny." **– Matthew 5:21-26**

ANGER MANAGEMENT

Day 8: Anger Management

Some say the opposite of love is not hate, but apathy. Regardless of the polar placements of love and hate Jesus makes it very clear as to what our attitude should be regarding both. We are to love what is good and hate what is evil. We are to love our brothers and NOT hate our enemies.

Be Reconciled

Anger is like a poisonous root that if left unchecked will grow causing bitterness and defiling everyone around it. A common misconception is the notion that if you give full vent to anger it will dissipate. However, anger does not work that way. In fact, the more you give into anger the angrier you become. Therefore we are to make reconciliation a priority. God is deaf to the hearts that are full of anger, bitterness and hate. How can we even possibly claim to love God while simultaneously hating our brother? John calls this person a liar.

Settle Matters Quickly

No one likes a drawn out struggle. Court cases happen on a daily basis dealing with many grievances against others. Do we have time to devote to these kinds of civilian affairs? Additionally, what message is conveyed when we are putting more faith in the legal system than in God? Our Father who sees our injustice will richly reward us. Paul even states, "why not rather be wronged." If it comes down to us and our brother, our hearts should be willing to be wronged for the sake of peace. James said the rich are dragging us into court. Is this not true? What should our hearts be toward those who are our adversaries?

Don't Grumble

"Stop grumbling among yourselves,' Jesus answered." – John 6:43

If we are not to grumble among ourselves, who should we grumble to? Notice how Jesus answered anyone who had a question about him or what he did even to those who were trying to trap him in his words. However, for those who were grumbling to themselves they would rather convince themselves that what they believe is true.

To such an attitude Jesus rebukes. When we grumble amongst each other against others, whether they are our brothers, leaders or even toward God, we cease to look for answers or help. A grumbling heart is a heart content with being angry and only seeks fuel to feed the anger. Jesus simply tells us to put a stop to it.

Reflection and Practical Application

1. Pray for a peaceful heart.
2. Reconcile any issues that are outstanding.
3. Practice humility by being first to apologize.

"But whoever lives by the truth comes into the light, so that it may be seen plainly that what he has done has been done through God."

– John 3:21

LIVING BY TRUTH

Day 9: Living By Truth

Run Into the Light

We are now in the light of Jesus because we desired to know and live by the truth. When people desire to deceive and live a life of deception, they refuse to come into the light. In fact, they will run from the light for fear of being exposed. Jesus freed us from a life of sin and shame. It is this sin that so easily entangles that Jesus warns us to stay away from because of its destructive and devastating consequences.

Let Your Yes Be Yes

"Again, you have heard that it was said to the people long ago, 'Do not break your oath, but keep the oaths you have made to the Lord.' But I tell you, Do not swear at all: either by heaven, for it is God's throne; or by the earth, for it is his footstool; or by Jerusalem, for it is the city of the Great King. And do not swear by your head, for you cannot make even one hair white or black. Simply let your 'Yes' be 'Yes,' and your 'No,' 'No'; anything beyond this comes from the evil one." – **Matthew 5:33-37**

Before we were called out of darkness our native language was deceit. In order for our words to have merit we would compound them with swearing and oaths. Now that we live by truth in the light we are simply able to let our 'Yes' be 'Yes' and our 'No' be 'No.'

Stop Sinning

"So they asked him, "Who is this fellow who told you to pick it up and walk?"

The man who was healed had no idea who it was, for Jesus had slipped away into the crowd that was there.

Later Jesus found him at the temple and said to him, "See, you are well again. Stop sinning or something worse may happen to you." – **John 5:12-14**

The net result of sin is death and between desire and death there are a host of consequences that we would rather avoid. Jesus warns this man of a fate worse than his previous condition. When we repent and confess our sins, we find healing and forgiveness. To understand the mind controlled by sin is to understand the reasons a man would risk living in a worse condition than what he was healed from. How grateful are we that our sins are forgiven? To lose that gratitude is to risk slipping further away from the grace of God that healed us.

Cut Off Sin

"Woe to the world because of the things that cause people to sin! Such things must come, but woe to the man through whom they come! If your hand or your foot causes you to sin, cut it off and throw it away. It is better for you to enter life maimed or crippled than to have two hands or two feet and be thrown into eternal fire. And if your eye causes you to sin, gouge it out and throw it away. It is better for you to enter life with one eye than to have two eyes and be thrown into the fire of hell." – **Matthew 18:7-9**

Many debates have formed around Jesus' words regarding the seriousness of sin. Jesus commands us not to grumble amongst ourselves and this would be a passage ripe for grumbling. Are we to literally cut off a hand or foot? Do we gouge out an eye? If we were diagnosed with cancer and it was in our hand or foot or eye, we would not hesitate to have it cut off and thrown away. We would not ask to see it afterward or feel a certain attachment to it. It caused us too much pain to warrant sentiment – we are only relieved to be rid of it so that we may live. Unfortunately, we focus more on losing our body parts, rather than being freed from sin. Sin is a cancerous death dealing disease and to not take such a radical stand against it is to miss the sacrifice of the cross. Fear not, however, our hands, feet and eyes do not cause us to sin. Is Jesus being literal? Yes. Jesus says, "If" and we know that it is not what's on the outside that causes sin, but what comes from within – our hearts.

Lust and Adultery

"You have heard that it was said, 'Do not commit adultery. 'But I tell you that anyone who looks at a woman lustfully has already committed adultery with her in his heart. If your right eye causes you to sin, gouge it out and throw it away. It is better for you to lose one part of your body than for your whole body to be thrown into hell. And if your right hand causes you to sin, cut it off and throw it away. It is better for you to lose one part of your body than for your whole body to go into hell." – **Matthew 5:27-30**

How is lust different from adultery? According to Jesus' words, they are exactly the same. Why then, do so many religious people judge the adulterous or divorced person so harshly? Outward actions will always be easier to see than the inner workings of the heart. Outwardly I appear healthy with an average weight for my height. Inwardly I wrestle with eating healthy and portion control. Do I receive unsolicited critical advice or harsh judgment regarding my diet and exercise – absolutely not. Yet a person with far more discipline who has a different outward appearance will find themselves at the receiving end of such poor judgment.

Jesus addresses a heart issue that causes religious self-righteousness. Jesus is helping his followers to avoid the path of hypocrisy and Pharisee attitude that condemns one form of sin, but willingly accepts or tolerates another form. If we are to be indignant about righteousness, that indignation should first be applied to our own hearts. Righteous indignation toward others is without having first a deep self-reflection never amounts to a recipe for successful Christian living.

Divorce

"It has been said, 'Anyone who divorces his wife must give her a certificate of divorce.' But I tell you that anyone who divorces his wife, except for marital unfaithfulness, causes her to become an adulteress, and anyone who marries the divorced woman commits adultery." – Matthew 5:31-32

Jesus again is addressing our hearts toward sin. It is our hearts that start us on our journey toward sinning in our actions. Jesus does not separate the two. Jesus knows once sin has taken hold of our hearts that our actions will surely follow.

Reflection and Practical Application

1. Get with your discipling partner and confess your sins.
2. Think of someone you know who has not been freed from those sins.
3. Pray for them and pray that God will give you an opportunity to share your faith so they may be healed.

"As Jesus started on his way, a man ran up to him and fell on his knees before him. "Good teacher," he asked, "what must I do to inherit eternal life?"

"Why do you call me good?" Jesus answered. "No one is good—except God alone. You know the commandments: 'Do not murder, do not commit adultery, do not steal, do not give false testimony, do not defraud, honor your father and mother.' "

"Teacher," he declared, "all these I have kept since I was a boy."

Jesus looked at him and loved him. "One thing you lack," he said. "Go, sell everything you have and give to the poor, and you will have treasure in heaven. Then come, follow me." **– Matthew 19:17-21**

TOP TEN

Day 10: Top Ten

Obey the Commandments

When the Rich Young Ruler encountered Jesus he asked what he must do to have eternal life. In some ways it appears as if the rich young man desired to add to his vast wealth by sealing it with immortality. Regardless of his reasoning Jesus tells the young man to obey the Ten Commandments. Interesting to note, Jesus only mentions six of the Ten Commandments. The other four are almost assumed – implying the commonality of obeying them.

However, for this rich young man it was not his moral failures that kept him from the kingdom of God, it was his trust in wealth. Amazingly, the rich young man was able to confidently say he had and could obey the Old Testament commands. However, Jesus was not interested in the man's ability to follow rules. Jesus was deeply interested in knowing if the young man could trust God with his life.

For the rich young man, his possessions and wealth equated to his life. It was how he felt secure from hunger or danger or threats from others who would exploit him or take advantage of him. Jesus was telling this man to let go of this other god and put your trust in the only true God. Unfortunately, we know the end of the story, the young man walks away disappointed.

The Greatest Command

"Hearing that Jesus had silenced the Sadducees, the Pharisees got together. One of them, an expert in the law, tested him with this question:

"Teacher, which is the greatest commandment in the Law?" Jesus replied: " 'Love the Lord your God with all your heart and with all your soul and with all your mind.' This is the first and greatest commandment. And the second is like it: 'Love your neighbor as yourself.' All the Law and the Prophets hang on these two commandments." – Matthew 22:34-40

How is greatness defined? We typically see an ordered list and assume the first or the last item on the list is the most important.

Equally, we may see repetition as an emphasis for what is the greater of a selection. However, greatness of the commands is not defined this way. Jesus points out the greatest command while most teachers of the Law failed to discover. Loving God is the greatest command.

Without love at the center of our faith, worship and life then we have failed at obeying the commands of God. It is as if every other act of obedience to God's commands are nullified in this one act of disobedience. It is no wonder why Jesus could be so hard on the Pharisees who obeyed more commands than others and yet have so much compassion on "sinners" who obeyed only a few commands.

Reflection and Practical Application

1. Write down how you love God with your heart.
2. Write down also how you love God with your mind, soul and strength (each separately).
3. Think of creative ways in each category to do so even more with one new action today.

Part Two: GROWING IN THE GRACE

WEEK **THREE**

"On hearing this, Jesus said, "It is not the healthy who need a doctor, but the sick. But go and learn what this means: 'I desire mercy, not sacrifice.' For I have not come to call the righteous, but sinners."

– Matthew 9:12-13.

KNOW MERCY

Day 11: Know Mercy

We are to learn what it means to be merciful to the extent of its importance above and beyond sacrifice. To show and have mercy is not simply showing kindness. The word "mercy" is commonly defined as "compassionate treatment especially to an offender." Jesus uses the Good Samaritan as an example of a person showing mercy. The Samaritan was looked down at as less in the eyes of a Jewish person because they were no longer considered children of Abraham. Therefore, for a Samaritan to show mercy to a Jewish man demonstrated a heart of mercy because he had never been on the receiving end of mercy from a Jewish man.

Show Mercy

"Just then a religion scholar stood up with a question to test Jesus. "Teacher, what do I need to do to get eternal life?"

He answered, "What's written in God's Law? How do you interpret it?"

He said, "That you love the Lord your God with all your passion and prayer and muscle and intelligence—and that you love your neighbor as well as you do yourself."

"Good answer!" said Jesus. "Do it and you'll live."

Looking for a loophole, he asked, "And just how would you define 'neighbor'?"

Jesus answered by telling a story. "There was once a man traveling from Jerusalem to Jericho. On the way he was attacked by robbers. They took his clothes, beat him up, and went off leaving him half-dead. Luckily, a priest was on his way down the same road, but when he saw him he angled across to the other side. Then a Levite religious man showed up; he also avoided the injured man.

"A Samaritan traveling the road came on him. When he saw the man's condition, his heart went out to him. He gave him first aid, disinfecting and bandaging his wounds. Then he lifted him onto his donkey, led him to an inn, and made him comfortable. In the morning he took out two silver coins and gave them to the innkeeper, saying, 'Take good care of him. If it costs any more, put it on my bill—I'll pay you on my way back.'

"What do you think? Which of the three became a neighbor to the man attacked by robbers?" – **Luke 10:27-36 (MSG)**

"The expert in the law replied, "The one who had mercy on him."

Jesus told him, "Go and do likewise." – **Luke 10:37 (NIV)**

Love Your Enemies

"You have heard that it was said, 'Love your neighbor and hate your enemy.' But I tell you: Love your enemies and pray for those who persecute you, that you may be sons of your Father in heaven. He causes his sun to rise on the evil and the good, and sends rain on the righteous and the unrighteous. If you love those who love you, what reward will you get? Are not even the tax collectors doing that? And if you greet only your brothers, what are you doing more than others? Do not even pagans do that? Be perfect, therefore, as your heavenly Father is perfect." – **Matthew 5:43-48**

Often we associate love with an emotion we feel as we act lovingly toward someone. However, this is not the case. We may feel love from someone and therefore have a good feeling as we show them love in return, but true love includes sacrifice. Jesus was filled with joy as he set out to die on the cross. However, there is no indication that Jesus felt the feelings of love as he was flogged, beaten and crucified. We know that this was God's greatest act of love toward us, but we know it also was devastating to endure. To show love to someone who is our enemy is the same love God showed us. We were all God's enemies when Jesus went to die for our sins, yet God showed us his love just the same. We are being called to be imitators of God in this way.

Pray for Your Enemies

Jesus prayed for his enemies. Again, we were all once enemies of God and Jesus prayed for us even before we were born or came to believe in him (John 17:20). How incredible is it that Jesus would pour out his heart to God for a group of people who he knew would curse, slander, ridicule and take for granted every act of kindness he had ever committed. Many of us search to find strength to pray. Still more of us need a reason to pray for others. And finally, the majority of us have to pray for our own hearts to expend the type of energy Jesus had in his prayers for his enemies.

We were Jesus' enemies. We are no longer. Think about the people we keep in our dungeon of judgment and lack of forgiveness. Now imagine their hearts moved by prayer to true change and repentance. This has been the power of Jesus' prayer for our lives. We are called to imitate Jesus' heart in praying for our enemies. If we have faith, we believe they will not always be our enemies.

Bless Your Enemies

We may be able to show love and even pray for our enemies, but bless them? Paul said when we were cursed we blessed. How often do we respond with blessings when we are wronged? When someone cuts me off while driving and then slows down (for the life of me I will never understand this) I don't immediately feel in my heart,

Day 11: Know Mercy / 73

"let me bless them." On the contrary, if we were to see this same car pulled over by a state trooper and getting ticket for reckless driving, somewhere in our hearts we would feel the slightest joy of justice being served. Our initial response to cursing is a demand for justice. In fact, we call out to God for justice. We desire God to see our circumstances and act on our behalf so that those who deserve punishment get what they rightly deserve. However, how often to do we call for justice for our own actions? What would justice for our actions against Jesus look like? Our actions and desire to live free from God's is the very reason Jesus was sent to take our place on the cross. If being crucified on a wooden beam with nails driven into our hands and feet justice for our actions – would we still demand it? What we truly desire is not justice, but mercy. Jesus showed us mercy by taking our punishment for us. The sin that brought him punishment are now the wounds that bring us peace (Isaiah 53:5).

Be Perfect

Is Jesus commanding us to do the impossible? No. Many assume to obtain perfection we must work and earn a level of righteousness in order to be viewed by God as good or holy. This is a futile effort and not even Job who was considered to be the most righteous man to ever live could stand before God blameless. We are called to His standard and not our own standard of righteousness. Jesus gives us one simple truth to obey in order to be perfect. Jesus says, "If you want to be perfect, go, sell your possessions and give to the poor, and you will have treasure in heaven. Then come, follow me"

(Matthew 19:21 NIV). Perfection can never be obtained by following a set of rules. Perfection can only be obtained by following Jesus.

Reflection and Practical Application

1. Think of ways to be more merciful in your day
    a. As you drive
    b. As you work
    c. As you interact with family.
2. Show someone that has offended you unmerited kindness.
3. Pray for them.

"You have heard that it was said, 'Eye for eye, and tooth for tooth.' But I tell you, Do not resist an evil person. If someone strikes you on the right cheek, turn to him the other also. And if someone wants to sue you and take your tunic, let him have your cloak as well. If someone forces you to go one mile, go with him two miles. Give to the one who asks you, and do not turn away from the one who wants to borrow from you."

– Matthew 5:38-42

Day 12: The Extra Mile

In a world that promotes so many liberties and individual rights we can often become baffled at Jesus' words that tell us to do the opposite of what makes sense. We should pummel evil people and vanquish them at every turn. If someone strikes us, we should defend ourselves and make sure we strike back harder. If someone wants to sue us, we make sure we take them to the cleaners. And lastly, if someone forces us to do anything (one mile or two), we make sure they know about it in the most colorful language. It is no wonder that Jesus calls us to give up everything we have first to follow him because this is what we live to protect. We want to protect our lives and things. **How can we possibly expect to live out any more of Jesus' commands if we cannot begin with the first of his words?**

Left and Right Hand

"Be careful not to do your 'acts of righteousness' before men, to be seen by them. If you do, you will have no reward from your Father in heaven.

"So when you give to the needy, do not announce it with trumpets, as the hypocrites do in the synagogues and on the streets, to be honored by men. I tell you the truth, they have received their reward in full. But when you give to the needy, do not let your left hand know what your right hand is doing, so that your giving may be in secret. Then your Father, who sees what is done in secret, will reward you." – Matthew 6:1-4

For some, the concept of desiring praise for a good deed is so foreign that to be told not to boast about a kind act seems almost nonsensical. This is a "left hand" not knowing what "the right hand" is doing. It is when Jesus calls us to account for an act of kindness at judgment and we say, "When did we see you poor, naked or in prison?" However, the hypocrite (pretender) has no future hope and desires an earthly reward so they announce everything they do in media and to anyone who will listen.

Do Unto Others

"So in everything, do to others what you would have them do to you, for this sums up the Law and the Prophets." – **Matthew 7:12**

"Then Jesus said to his host, "When you give a luncheon or dinner, do not invite your friends, your brothers or relatives, or your rich neighbors; if you do, they may invite you back and so you will be repaid. But when you give a banquet, invite the poor, the crippled, the lame, the blind, and you will be blessed. Although they cannot repay you, you will be repaid at the resurrection of the righteous." – **Luke 14:12-14**

Many of us are familiar with corrupt politics. We hear of officials using power to gain wealth and receiving wealth to turn a blind eye to justice. Hypocrites also do this with the hidden motive to receive. They throw lavish banquets so they can impress their friends. They desire to be welcomed in the homes of the rich and curry favor for later use. As foreigners of this world we await a King and Savior from our true home and our actions are also foreign to the residents of this place. We give with no hidden agenda and we serve without thought of repayment.

Reflection and Practical Application

1. As ambassadors of Christ we represent him in every way. In what ways have you positively represented Christ?
2. Make every effort to serve and give as Jesus would without pomp, recognition or praise.

3. Plan to have hospitality for a few guests after church service or a date night. Do it with a cheerful heart expecting only praise from God.

"Enter through the narrow gate. For wide is the gate and broad is the road that leads to destruction, and many enter through it. But small is the gate and narrow the road that leads to life, and only a few find it."

– Matthew 7:13-14.

Day 13: The Way

A command of Jesus: "Enter through the narrow gate." There are only two commands for those who have lost their way, "Repent and be baptized and repent and pray." For us, entering through the narrow gate is determining that we will constantly bear fruit of repentance. We must persevere to the end.

The Narrow Gate

In trying to imagine the kind of visual Jesus is using is to think about how wide toll roads become at the point the cars cross the payment gates. A six to eight lane highway quickly turns into a 20 lane highway. You can look left and right and see cars spread out over lane after lane. This is the broad road. This is the number Jesus wants us to get in our minds of just how many people are driving along through life oblivious. Think about the vastness of cars going through one after another as we travel by in our "cash only" lane that no one wants to be in. This is the kind of urgency Jesus wants us to have regarding salvation for ourselves and salvation for others.

Reflection and Practical Application

1. Determine to keep in step with the Spirit and live a life that constantly bears fruit for God.
2. Determine to repent of sin quickly, openly and with deep conviction and indignation.
3. Warn those who you know are traveling down the broad road with love, compassion and sincerity.

"Then he said to his disciples, "The harvest is plentiful but the workers are few. Ask the Lord of the harvest, therefore, to send out workers into his harvest field." – **Matthew 9:37, 38.**

"After this the Lord appointed seventy-two others and sent them two by two ahead of him to every town and place where he was about to go. He told them, "The harvest is plentiful, but the workers are few. Ask the Lord of the harvest, therefore, to send out workers into his harvest field. Go! I am sending you out like lambs among wolves." – **Luke 10:1-3.**

"My food," said Jesus, "is to do the will of him who sent me and to finish his work. Do you not say, 'Four months more and then the harvest'? I tell you, open your eyes and look at the fields! They are ripe for harvest." – **John 4:34-35.**

THE HARVEST IS PLENTIFUL

Day 14: The Harvest is Plentiful

Jesus gives us two commands here. The first is to ask God, who is Lord of the harvest, for workers. The second is like the first, which is to "Go" into the harvest fields. Ironically, Jesus is saying we are the answer to our prayers. First we pray and then we go!

To imagine Jesus' resolve to do the will of the Father is to imagine being consumed with something so deeply that food is a distant second or afterthought. Jesus' disciples urged Jesus to eat something, but Jesus responded by saying his food is to do the will of God. **Food is a basic need for every person** and we instinctively pursue it without much planning, forethought or effort. We are even actually creative in our pursuit of food and desire to vary our palate for interest.

"The laborer's appetite works for him; his hunger drives him on." – Proverbs 16:26.

If Jesus was referring to this passage in Proverbs he most likely was trying to get his disciples to understand the reason for his "fasting." Jesus' fast from food created a hunger and desire to complete God's will even before meeting his own basic need for food and sustenance.

Let Nothing Be Wasted

"When they had all had enough to eat, he said to his disciples, "Gather the pieces that are left over. Let nothing be wasted." – John 6:12.

On more than one occasion we see a command that references food or animals. These commands are to call our attention more to our relationship with one another or God's will than it is our treatment of food or animals. Paul references a command regarding muzzling the ox as a reference for a worker being worth his wages. Paul is saying that God is more concerned about the well-being of one of his servants more than that of a person's ox treading out grain.

Here Jesus is referring to food not being wasted which indeed has practical use, but I believe he is more concerned about God's will than the remaining loaves and fishes. In conjunction with being sent into the harvest field (which is a food analogy) we are to gather the harvest knowing that there is more work than workers. The net result is that if we who are called to be the workers fail to gather the harvest we are allowing a great waste to result.

Go Work in the Vineyard

"For the kingdom of heaven is like a landowner who went out early in the morning to hire men to work in his vineyard. He agreed to pay them a denarius for the day and sent them into his vineyard.

"About the third hour he went out and saw others standing in the marketplace doing nothing. He told them, 'You also go and work in my vineyard, and I will pay you whatever is right.' So they went." – Matthew 20:1-5.

The Lord has hired us to work in his vineyard. We were all at one point standing in the "marketplace" of life without purpose, doing nothing of significance. There is a great deal of work that needs to be done and most of us would understand if we were fired from a job if we occasional showed up for work or decided to work when we felt like it. Jesus did not have this work ethic for doing God's will. Jesus sets the ultimate example by prioritizing the will of God as most important, even beyond his own needs.

Reflection and Practical Application

1. Pray to God for more workers to be sent out into the harvest.
2. Determine to work with the same motivation and zeal that Jesus showed.

WEEK THREE

"These twelve Jesus sent out with the following instructions: "Do not go among the Gentiles or enter any town of the Samaritans. Go rather to the lost sheep of Israel. As you go, preach this message: 'The kingdom of heaven is near.' Heal the sick, raise the dead, cleanse those who have leprosy, drive out demons. Freely you have received, **freely give**."

— Matthew 10:5-8 (NIV)

FREELY GIVE

Day 15: Freely Give

Freely Give

We have received the gift of the Holy Spirit. Jesus commands that we freely give away what we have received from him. We have freely received the good news of the kingdom and with that a new purpose for our lives. We have freely received healing and freedom from sin. These are among the many blessings that we are commanded to give away freely – without charge.

Jesus speaking through Paul says, "It is more blessed to give than receive" (Acts 20:35 NIV). Some time ago a friend asked me what Jesus could have meant by this teaching. I asked him to imagine being given the choice to receive a brand new car or give one away. Then I asked him what would be better – which would make you happier? The obvious choice to him and to most people is the first choice. We can all imagine an "Oprah-like" moment where a frenzy of talk-show guests display euphoric happiness because they have just been given a brand new car (tax not included). However, we rarely think about how Oprah Winfrey felt giving away the cars to her audience.

What does this have to do with the blessing that comes from giving? It's simple, we can easily miss the blessing that we have that enables us to give generously. Not everyone will have the means to give away a car to an entire studio audience, but the principles are the same. The very act of giving helps us recognize how much God has blessed us. In Deuteronomy 8:18 we see in Scripture how God desires us to understand this concept by saying, "But remember the Lord your God, for it is he who gives you the ability to produce wealth."

Reflection and Practical Application

1. What are some ways in which you can be more generous?
2. Have you given to the point of being sacrificial?
3. Think of ways you can freely give: forgiveness, healing, and a life-changing gift.

week FOUR

"These twelve Jesus sent out, instructing them, "Go nowhere among the Gentiles and enter no town of the Samaritans, but go rather to the lost sheep of the house of Israel. And proclaim as you go, saying, 'The kingdom of heaven is at hand.' **Heal the sick**, raise the dead, cleanse lepers, cast out demons. You received without paying; give without pay."

– Matthew 10:5-8 (ESV)

Day 16: Heal the Sick

The condition of the world is spiritually sick. Though we often think of poor health and sickness in terms of physical health, we know that Jesus shows us earthly examples and lessons first before the spiritual. No doctor spends more time on patients who are healthy. If we look across the table at someone who is lost, we should see a spiritually sick person. Symptoms include: distrust, denial, greed, compulsive lying, envy, jealousy, strife, unbelief, abusive behavior (to others and to self), and the like.

Scriptures say that "hope deferred makes the heart sick" (Proverbs 13:12 ESV). What causes the massive epidemic of uncontained outbreak of spiritually sick people? Hope. Is hope the enemy? Of course not. It is the lack of hope that infects and festers in the hearts of people. Where do we find this disease? In the heart is where we find distrust, denial, greed and so on. The heart is the place where the condition of the spiritually sick can be cured or grow worse. Jesus says, "For out of the heart come evil thoughts, murder, adultery, sexual immorality, theft, false witness, slander" (Matthew 15:19, 20 ESV).

The rest of Proverbs 13:12 (ESV) reads, "but a desire fulfilled is a tree of life." What does a person desire in their heart of hearts? We find the answer to this question again in Proverbs – "what a person desires is unfailing love" (Proverbs 19:22 NIV). Everyone is searching for the kind of unfailing love that can only come from the gospel of Christ. The words of the gospel have true healing powers. Jesus says, "the words I have spoken to you are spirit and they are life" (John 6:63 NIV). Jesus' words have life-giving qualities that can heal the sick. Imagine feeling unconditional, unfailing love all the time – it would feel like a tree of life! People search intently for this feeling on earth, but it can only come from heaven. Which is why we know that God made our hearts to have a "God-shaped" hole in it that can only be filled by him.

Just Like Jesus

You would think with all these life-giving abilities that Jesus would go after large crowds and call us to do the same. However, Jesus didn't go after crowds. He used the crowds as an opportunity to teach his disciples. He spoke to the crowds as much as they could understand and explained deeper things to his disciples.

Jesus' primary focus in his ministry was to preach the word – the life-giving word of God to those who were closest to him – his disciples. These disciples, including us today, would change the world. What we find to be more consistent with Jesus' healing moments in his ministry were that they were more of a hindrance than a focus – it distracted him from training his disciples.

Lack of Understanding Creates a Hard Heart

"For they still didn't understand the significance of the miracle of the loaves. Their hearts were too hard to take it in." – Mark 6:52 (NLT).

With all that Jesus taught and did, there was still a disconnect with those who listened. Like any good medicine, it can only work if the patient "takes it in." Jesus performed miraculous signs for a reason and that significance escaped the disciples who could not make the spiritual connection between the loaves and the message of the gospel. When teaching in large crowds, Jesus noticed how many lacked understanding. To some extent this was his intention. He knew if they understood with their hearts, their hearts would soften and they would turn and be healed.

Some Regions are Evil

So they arrived at the other side of the lake, in the region of the Gerasenes. When Jesus climbed out of the boat, a man possessed by an evil [unclean] spirit came out from a cemetery to meet him.

A crowd soon gathered around Jesus, and they saw the man who had been possessed by the legion of demons. He was sitting there fully clothed and perfectly sane, and they were all afraid. Then those who had seen what happened told the others about the demon-possessed man and the pigs. And the crowd began pleading with Jesus to go away and leave them alone. – Mark 5:1-2, 15-17

Why would Jesus keep this life-giving message from anyone? Rather, a better question is why would anyone resist a message that could bring healing and life? The people pleaded with Jesus to leave their region, not because of the loss they had with the 2,000 pigs, but because of what they saw and heard Jesus do for the demon-possessed man.

You might imagine some conversations going something like this, "Did you see what he did to that insane man? Righteousness flows from this man like nothing we've ever seen. He will turn our towns upside down if we let him stay."

Why else would the demons plead with Jesus to allow them to stay in the region? Demons look for a place to rest. They surely felt at home in this region. Not a popular thing to say, but some regions are evil and will be resistant to the gospel message. We are called to heal, but we are warned to shake the dust if we find obstinacy (Luke 9:5).

The Pharisees Want to Kill Jesus

"So the Pharisees and teachers of the law asked Jesus, "Why don't your disciples live according to the tradition of the elders instead of eating their food with 'unclean' hands?"

He replied, "Isaiah was right when he prophesied about you hypocrites; as it is written: 'These people honor me with their lips, but their hearts are far from me. They worship me in vain; their teachings are but rules taught by men.' You have let go of the commands of God and are holding on to the traditions of men."

And he said to them: "You have a fine way of setting aside the commands of God in order to observe your own traditions! For Moses said, 'Honor your father and your mother,' and, 'Anyone who curses his father or mother must be put to death.' But you say that if a man says to his father or mother: 'Whatever help you might otherwise have received from me is Corban' (that is, a gift devoted to God), then you no longer let him do anything for his father or mother. Thus you nullify the word of God by your tradition that you have handed down. And you do many things like that." – Mark 7:5-13

Jesus makes a bold statement about the requirements of the law that the Pharisees are breaking. In fact, Jesus says, "Anyone who curses his father or mother must be put to death." If the crowds turning to Jesus realized that the Pharisees are dishonoring their fathers and mothers they could turn against them and demand they pay the penalty - death!

Why does the life-giving, healing power of the gospel also bring persecution? We see what controversy it stirred among the rigidly religious people of Jesus' day. These Pharisees were getting a dose of their own medicine. The same dogmatic arrogance that attempted to trap the Lord in his words with the woman caught in adultery are now feeling the brunt as the tables are turned against them by being confronted with the Law they so righteously claim to uphold.

The people praised God for giving such authority to men.

"When the crowd saw this, they were filled with awe; and they praised God, who had given such authority to men." – Matthew 9:8

Reflection and Practical Application

1. Do we use our authority to heal the sick like Jesus?
2. Do we feel empowered (authorized) to drive out the demons in the lives of people who need spiritual healing?
3. How often are we using our "authority" to pray and heal?
4. How often are we using our authority to rebuke and command evil to flee from the lives of our brothers and sisters or people we know?

Jesus sent his twelve harvest hands out with this charge: "Don't begin by traveling to some far-off place to convert unbelievers. And don't try to be dramatic by tackling some public enemy. Go to the lost, confused people right here in the neighborhood. Tell them that the kingdom is here. Bring health to the sick. Raise the dead. **Touch the untouchables**. Kick out the demons. You have been treated generously, so live generously." – Matthew 10:5-16 (MSG)

THE UNTOUCHABLES

Day 17: The Untouchables

I remember some time ago getting into a heated argument with my roommate because I had shown kindness to a stranger. This stranger was a homeless person with HIV and I had let him use our shower and towels. Now mind you I had washed the towels after they were used. This did not matter to my roommate. He wanted me to identify the towels so that he could discard them. I assumed he wanted to burn them, place them in their own garbage bag and call for a special trash pick-up.

Why do we feel this way about our own personal towels, yet we pay to dry off with towels that have been used by thousands of people at fancy hotels? Our standards are amazingly inconsistent. My roommate nearly blew a gasket because I had offered this man a chance to get clean and wash his clothes. It was terribly difficult to refuse because he made a humble request. He wanted to visit his mother in the hospital but did not want her to see him in his disheveled state. Compassion welled up in my heart. In Chicago, where most of my requests end with money or at the most food, I decided to grant this man's appeal and I treated him as I would a brother. I fed him and clothed him and sent him on his way.

I could tell he was suffering from an illness and he confirmed it by letting me know right away that he was HIV positive. There was a moment where he paused believing I would accept this opportunity to get out of my offer. I did not. Instead, I motioned him toward my home. Although I had learned enough about HIV and how it cannot be transmitted by touch it did not change the very real feeling of dread as I looked on the man's face and saw open scars. I thought to myself, "Do open scars present a danger to me?" I dismissed the thought and subjected my fears to my sense of duty because I held the ability to do something about his request.

Jesus often healed those who had a wasting skin disease and the mere sight of someone with this condition would send alarms in our minds to keep our distance. Touching them would surely mean we would contract the same disease. We find law after law in Leviticus describing the legal proceedings necessary for a person with any type of skin disease. They must keep away from others, they should yell, "unclean!"

The power of the human touch is so incredible. To imagine a group of people who have gone without the caring touch of another human being is unthinkable. We hug, we shake hands, we push, we embrace, we kiss, we mess up hair, we punch shoulders – we touch. We need the comforting love of touch. Newborn babies need it. We give it every day and we need it every day. We believe we have nothing to give to the homeless person on the street because we do not have money, but we do – we have touch. And they need it from us who have the power to give.

Reflection and Practical Application

1. Determine to give more than just monetarily.
2. Find a needy person and comfort them.
3. Think of others who could benefit from a hug from you today.

"Cure the sick, **raise the dead**, cleanse the lepers, drive out demons. Freely (without pay) you have received, freely (without charge) give." – Matthew 10:8

RAISE THE DEAD

Day 18: Raise the Dead

Where certain needs will require healing other situations will require a complete spiritual resurrection. Some are walking zombies and are dead spiritually. Jesus called some Pharisees white washed tombs full of dead men's bones. Even in such a spiritual state, God has given us freely the power to raise these people back to life again through the gospel and the power of the Holy Spirit.

Jesus was the first person to recognize the walking dead. In Luke 9:63 Jesus says, "let the dead bury their own dead." How do the dead do anything? This is a remarkable comparison. There are two groups of people Jesus refers to: the physically dead and the spiritually dead. However, in one sentence Jesus groups the two into one descriptive word – "dead." The reality of spiritual death was alarming to Jesus. Therefore Jesus used words to convey the same alarm to his hearers. To be spiritually dead was to be a living, breathing zombie. Spiritual death *is* death. We are in a real end-of-the-world horror movie surrounded by zombies. The major difference is we have the power to resurrect the dead.

The seemingly wealthy, successful and carefree people we see everyday are wearing a disguise that desperately tries to hide the decaying condition of their souls. Proverbs 14:13 says, "even in laughter the heart may ache and joy may end in grief." Many happy faces mask the grotesque and disfigured soul.

Jesus calls us to proclaim the kingdom – it has the power to raise the dead.

Reflection and Practical Application

1. Think of people you know that appear to "have it all." Make a list of their names.
2. Pray for their spiritual resurrection.
3. Make it a goal to reach out to someone who is trapped by wealth and possessions. Share with them Jesus' perspective on the "walking dead."

"These twelve Jesus sent out with the following instructions: "Do not go among the Gentiles or enter any town of the Samaritans. Go rather to the lost sheep of Israel. As you go, preach this message: 'The kingdom of heaven is near.' Heal the sick, raise the dead, cleanse those who have leprosy,
drive out demons. Freely you have received, freely give."

– Matthew 10:5-8 (NIV)

DRIVE OUT DEMONS

Day 19: Drive out Demons

When there is no spiritual death or sickness, there can be possession. Demonic forces are at work in those who are disobedient and rebellious toward God. In their minds they are free, but in their souls they are slaves. We are called to free them from their bondage.

One of the many reasons I shy away from owning rental property is because of bad tenants. I used to be a bad tenant and I would never rent property to me. Before you start getting any ideas, I didn't destroy property or throw loud parties. However, I complained – a lot. Refrigerator needs replacing, the back door is drafty, there's a weird smell coming from the kitchen sink, and so on and so on. This would drive me crazy – don't call me! All demons are bad tenants and apparently they do throw parties. According to Scripture if you kick one demon out without getting a good tenant, they will come back with seven friends and throw a kegger (that is a party with a large container of beer central to the festivities). We are called to kick demons out, literally drive them out.

I have never had to deal with a bad tenant, but I can hardly imagine one that I would have to physically kick out of the apartment. The process of eviction is fairly civil: you get a notice, you get time to respond, you get your stuff put on the curb. Having bad tenants just seems like an unwelcomed headache.

Although some of us may imagine some sort of exorcism that should be performed in order to drive out demons, we are not dealing with the sensational version of this effort. Demons are simply the unclean spirits that are at work in those who are disobedient and rebellious to God. Demons find rest in these homes. It is the power of the gospel that fills cleaned homes (repented hearts) with a new tenant – the Holy Spirit.

Jesus desires to live in our heart of a home. Driving out demons is not a movie-like utterance of the same sentence repeated over and over. It is the patient preaching of the gospel that pushes out the demonic forces that enslave people to all types of vices.

Reflection and Practical Application

1. Have you ever encountered someone you thought was demon-possessed?
2. Did you avoid this person or think they needed help from the gospel?
3. Have you ever thought compulsive behavior is a sign of demon-possession?
4. How can the gospel help someone with compulsive or addictive behavior?

"I am sending you out like sheep among wolves. Therefore **be as shrewd as snakes and as innocent as doves**. Be on your guard; you will be handed over to the local councils and be flogged in the synagogues. On my account you will be brought before governors and kings as witnesses to them and to the Gentiles. But when they arrest you, do not worry about what to say or how to say it. At that time you will be given what to say, for it will not be you speaking, but the Spirit of your Father speaking through you." – **Matthew 10:16-19 (NIV)**

"Behold, I am sending you out like sheep in the midst of wolves; **be wary and wise as serpents, and be innocent (harmless, guileless, and without falsity) as doves**." – **Matthew 10:16 (AMP)**

SHREWD YET INNOCENT

Day 20: Shrewd Yet Innocent

As with any good physician you must have a good bedside manner. As children respond better when given candy, so certain patients respond better to a frightening procedure with added care and attention. We have to have a plan of attack and approach. Force fed medicine will often be rejected and waste time on both sides. When we give our entire heart to working in God's harvest field, we will put forth all our efforts to be as effective as possible in our approach.

Shrewd as Snakes, Innocent as Doves

For whatever reason when I imagine a character that is shrewd, yet innocent, I think of Tweety Bird. This cute innocent yellow bird with an unusually large head always found himself under the attack of Sylvester the cat. Surprisingly, this little bird could give as good as he would get. Tweety Bird would utterly devastate Sylvester with some cleverly crafted plan of counter-attack. Afterwards, Tweety would giggle, smile and bashfully drag his ridiculously large foot in front of his leg.

Tweety Bird meets much of the description of an innocent dove found in the Amplified text. It is true he meets the bird criteria, but more importantly he is "without falsity." Granted, there was nothing "harmless" about Tweety as other biblical translations render this passage. However, we should encompass all these attributes: innocent, harmless, guileless, and without falsity while demonstrating a strategic and intelligent approach to preaching the gospel.

"Harmless" also implies stealth like attributes. There are advantages to being unnoticed? Jesus on more than a few occasions desired to remain unnoticed and hidden. "[Jesus] entered a house and did not want anyone to know it; yet he could not keep his presence secret" (Mark 7:24 NIV). Previous chapters in the gospel of Mark reveal Jesus' motives to being hidden.

Just after Jesus heals a man with leprosy he gave him this instruction: "See that you don't tell this to anyone. But go, show yourself to the priest and offer the sacrifices that Moses commanded for your cleansing, as a testimony to them. Instead he went out and began to talk freely, spreading the news. As a result, Jesus could no longer enter a town openly but stayed outside in lonely places" (Mark 1:44, 45). Being harmless is to be considered irrelevant or non-threatening. Anything we consider non-threatening, we tend to ignore, thereby making the object nearly invisible to our radar.

The result of Jesus' popularity attracted crowds which prevented him from appearing openly in towns to teach. It would appear that such publicity would be welcomed and even useful to promote the efforts of Jesus' ministry. However, Jesus makes a distinction between spreading news about his miracles and spreading the gospel message. Jesus embodied the innocent, stealth, and unassuming presence of a dove in his ministry while passionately pursuing a shrewd strategy to preach in each town he went.

There are two emotional reactions when a snake is close to a person versus a dove. The snake immediately invokes a sense of alarm, fear, weariness and caution. We are keenly aware of the snake's presence, guarded and our senses are heightened. On the other hand, the dove has such a harmless characteristic that we not only do not fear the bird, but we are careful with our own actions toward it so as to not frighten the animal. The dove causes us to let down our guard. The snake makes us afraid.

When we say that we love God with all our heart, mind, soul and strength – I think of this passage. The Lord wants us to use our intelligence. He gave us our minds to use for his glory. Many activities that we are passionate about we tend to put all of our heart into it. We even speak this way, "I gave it all my heart." However, how often do we reflect on giving our entire mind to the glory of God? Do we give all of our attention for the needs of the kingdom?

Many things in our day take up our collective thought. We give careful attention to projects at work, our children's education, planning our retirement and other future prospects. What percentage of all this creative and intelligent thinking do we devote to proclaiming the kingdom? The level of strategic thinking that is involved in planning a global effort to reach the entire population is hard to fathom. Jesus' mission to transform the world would be alarming and unwelcomed by the religious majority. He would have to be shrewd in his approach.

Similarly, it must be difficult for high-ranking executives of major marketing brands to develop a strategy to increase market share without a high-level of confidentiality and planning. Loving God with all of our minds means applying more planning efforts toward our work in the kingdom than we would any other work-related project. We spend hours a week devoted to projects at work – a great deal of time dedicated to strategic thinking to promote the agendas of companies and CEOs. What should our percentage of intellectual devotion be toward God? It can only be one number according to Jesus – 100.

Reflection and Practical Application

1. Spend time making plans for being more effective in sharing your faith.
2. List the many blessings given to you by God.
3. Think of the ways others brought the gospel to you.
4. Think of ways to freely share your gifts with others.

Part Three: DANGEROUS AND UNLAWFUL

WEEK FIVE

"Be on your guard against men ...

So do not be afraid of them ... What I tell you in the dark, speak in the daylight; what is whispered in your ear, proclaim from the roofs. **Do not be afraid** of those who kill the body but cannot kill the soul. Rather, be afraid of the One who can destroy both soul and body in hell. Are not two sparrows sold for a penny? Yet not one of them will fall to the ground apart from the will of your Father. And even the very hairs of your head are all numbered. **So don't be afraid**; you are worth more than many sparrows." – Matthew 10:17-31.

HAVE NO FEAR

Day 21: Have No Fear

Not Afraid of ...

A Command: Do Not Fear

Of all the things that are expected in this Christian walk, the most certain of these is persecution. When we are face to face with persecution we find Jesus' words standing out to us with vibrant clarity. **If we label criticism as persecution and it does not have the quality to make us afraid or fearful of speaking, we are most likely mislabeling it persecution.** Persecution is intended to get us to act in such a way so that we are fearful of standing for Jesus and righteousness.

Persecution in Jesus' day was done by the religious leaders of the first-century to anyone who professed to believe in Jesus. Some even followed Jesus secretly because they feared being persecuted by the Pharisees – the consequence was being thrown out of the synagogue. If you are in an environment that uses coercion, tactics, or any practice that intimidates you to compromise righteousness, thoughts or opinions, then you are being persecuted. This environment may be a city, country, government or a religious group of people. Jesus calls us to not be afraid.

Reflection and Practical Application

1. Think of situations that make you afraid of sharing the gospel.
2. Determine to be unafraid as you confront this weakness.

"Blessed are you when men hate you, when they exclude you and insult you and reject your name as evil, because of the Son of Man.

Rejoice in that day and leap for joy, because great is your reward in heaven. For that is how their fathers treated the prophets."

– Luke 6:22-23

SOME THINGS ARE CERTAIN

Day 22: Some Things are Certain

Persecution, Death and Taxes

Persecution does not simply happen to anyone who wears a cross or quietly makes Jesus Lord. There is a direct connection between proclaiming Jesus and persecution. Persecution happens as a direct result of speaking in the daylight and proclaiming the gospel from the rooftops. Silent 'Christians' don't face persecution because they are silent. They go to church, they offer money for the collection, they take communion, they volunteer, they give to the poor, they treat their neighbors with kindness and respect, and they even go on mission trips to help the less fortunate in third world countries. What's missing? Proclaiming Jesus as the Christ and taking a vocal stand against unrighteousness. As a result, those who hate the light and righteousness will respond with persecution; starting from mild intimidation to violent threats of death. Jesus tells us to rejoice when this happens. We are not only called to be bold and unafraid, but to also rejoice. We have been counted worthy to suffer for the gospel!

Rejoice Under Persecution

Still, how did the apostles and early disciples rejoice under persecution? They counted themselves worthy because they realized their message was becoming recognized by the majority rule. In other words, their preaching was starting to get to people and was therefore a sign that the message of the gospel was growing and spreading rapidly (Acts 6:7 NIV).

Reflection and Practical Application

1. What are your greatest fears?
2. Pray for boldness and an opportunity to rejoice in the face of persecution.
3. Pray for those who slander, belittle, malign, defame, vilify or mock you.
4. Pray also for those who would do you harm for the sake of the gospel and righteousness.

"Whoever acknowledges me before men, I will also acknowledge him before my Father in heaven. But whoever disowns me before men, I will disown him before my Father in heaven." – **Matthew 10:32, 33.**

"If anyone is ashamed of me and my words, the Son of Man will be ashamed of him when he comes in his glory and in the glory of the Father and of the holy angels." – **Luke 9:26**

"If anyone is ashamed of me and my words in this adulterous and sinful generation, the Son of Man will be ashamed of him when he comes in his Father's glory with the holy angels." – **Mark 8:38**

UNASHAMED

Day 23: Unashamed

Try to imagine the set of circumstances that would cause you to deny Christ. Would you be tempted to deny your devotion to Jesus in front of a firing squad? Would the threat of imprisonment or torture be convincing tools to purchase your betrayal? Some situations are just discomforting enough to get us to simply remain silent and not speak of Jesus when we know we should. This is being ashamed of Jesus and his words.

We are afraid of what people will think or say or do. Just so there is no surprise, the mystery revealed is simply this: People will shun us, ridicule and hate us. If disciples are not properly prepared with these words they will be ill-equipped to face persecution when it comes.

"For God did not give us a spirit of timidity, but a spirit of power, of love and of self-discipline. So do not be ashamed to testify about our Lord, or ashamed of me his prisoner. **But join with me in suffering for the gospel**, by the power of God" – 2 Timothy 1:7, 8 (NIV).

Persecution is guaranteed if we are walking in the path of Christ. Persecution has a direct connection to the Great Commission – to "go." **Our circumstance causes us to engage in many of the "one another" commands we are called to do** by simply obeying a single command – to "go." As we go we face persecution because we are testifying to the truth. We are drawn closer to God because our situation causes us to rely on him as we attempt our impossible task of preaching the gospel to all nations and making disciples out of those who hear the message.

We are drawn to each other in fellowship because we are undergoing the same trials as our brothers and sisters all over the world. Quicker friendships are rarely found outside of a "fox-hole" friendship. In "fox-hole" friendships we share the same sufferings of persecution. We are immediately bonded by our shared circumstances. And where does all this begin? It starts as we follow in the footsteps of Christ.

Reflection and Practical Application

1. Make a decision to join your brothers and sisters all over the world in proclaiming the gospel.
2. Pray to be filled with boldness and power through the Holy Spirit.
3. Resolve to never be ashamed of Jesus and his words no matter what the circumstance.

"Then John's disciples came and asked him, "How is it that we and the Pharisees fast, but your disciples do not fast?"

Jesus answered, "How can the guests of the bridegroom mourn while he is with them? The time will come when the bridegroom will be taken from them; then they will fast.

No one sews a patch of unshrunk cloth on an old garment, for the patch will pull away from the garment, making the tear worse. Neither do men pour new wine into old wineskins. If they do, the skins will burst, the wine will run out and the wineskins will be ruined. No, they pour new wine into new wineskins, and both are preserved." – Matthew 9:14-17.

Day 24: New Wine Skins

After John was put in prison there remained faithful disciples still in his ministry. Even though John preached to his disciples that Jesus was the Christ and that they should follow him, there were only a few who actually listened to John. The gospel writers do not record why some of John's disciples remained with John and some with Jesus. We do know that John experienced a crisis of faith as he was in prison because he sent disciples to question Jesus to see if he truly was the Christ.

In this verse John's disciples are taking a page from the Pharisees' handbook and begin to question Jesus about fasting. Jesus responds by telling them in short that **His ways and ministry are new ways** and to combine an "old" heart with the new purpose would ruin the two. This is also why Jesus calls us to give up everything we have. We forsake our old ways and we take on the ways of Jesus.

Flexible Containers

This analogy is somewhat elusive, but very appropriate because they involve the same material, but at different stages. The cloth is the same and the skins are the same. The material is in essence a piece of flesh used to hold wine. The flesh represents our hearts. Our hearts can either be soft and flexible or rigid and resistant. The wine represents the new ways and teachings of Jesus. If our hearts are rigid, then we have no room for Jesus' words to grow in our hearts. How can they produce 30, 60, or a 100 times what has been sown if there is no room for expansion?

Jesus does not contradict himself or the word of God. However, our hearts have distorted the word of God and his command. We have therefore made it "our ways" and in this way our hearts have become "old wineskin." So Jesus, appropriately, tells us to pour new wine into new wine skins – though at this time it is Jesus doing the pouring.

So what does Jesus desire from us in this analogy? **We are to be new wine skins to be used by God.** Old wine skins are rigid and will break with new wine. In the same way an old garment is "set in its ways" and will not flex or shrink like a new garment. This is how our hearts should be and always remain before God – soft and moldable.

Reflection and Practical Application

1. Pray for a soft and pure heart.
2. Think of "old wine skin" traditions from your past that have crept into your worship of God. Write them down.
3. Decide today to put these burdens to rest and lay them down at the cross.
4. Decide today to live a life of humility as you follow Jesus in the way he calls.

"Watch out for false prophets. They come to you in sheep's clothing, but inwardly they are ferocious wolves. By their fruit you will recognize them. Do people pick grapes from thornbushes, or figs from thistles? Likewise every good tree bears good fruit, but a bad tree bears bad fruit. A good tree cannot bear bad fruit, and a bad tree cannot bear good fruit. Every tree that does not bear good fruit is cut down and thrown into the fire. Thus, by their fruit you will recognize them.

"Not everyone who says to me, 'Lord, Lord,' will enter the kingdom of heaven, but only he who does the will of my Father who is in heaven. Many will say to me on that day, 'Lord, Lord, did we not prophesy in your name, and in your name drive out demons and perform many miracles?' Then I will tell them plainly, 'I never knew you. Away from me, you evildoers!'" – Matthew 7:15-23.

WATCH OUT!

Day 25: Watch Out!

What is spiritual fruit? John the Baptist describes fruit in relation to repentance (Luke 3:8). God (in Genesis) describes fruit in relation to being "fruitful" – that is to produce offspring. Jesus describes fruit as that which holds the Word and the Word is the seed of the fruit. Paul describes fruit as the fruit of the Spirit (Galatians 5:22). Paul also describes the fruit of the Light (Ephesians 5:9).

Spiritual fruit has one overall marker – it is of God. Those who are godly will produce godly fruit and (according to Jesus) will do so abundantly. Fruit in its most general term is the product of that which bore it. An evil person produces fruit, but fruit for death. A righteous person produces fruit, but fruit for life, holiness, righteousness, goodness, love and the like. We bear fruit by reproducing the good that is in us. The Pharisees bore fruit, but it was considered "fruitless" because their fruit was twice as bad as they were. Therefore, whether it is in words, actions, deeds or converts, we will be able to recognize who is sent from God and who is not by their fruit.

By Their Fruit

Shockingly, there are people today who claim to be the second coming of Christ. Even more shocking are the number of followers these people have. The disciples on the road to Emmaus recognized Jesus because he opened their minds to understand the Word and their hearts burned within them. In addition to the Holy Spirit within us testifying to the truth of the word of God, we have discernment through the Word to see what kind of fruit they are bearing. If it looks like bad fruit, and talks like bad fruit, and walks like bad fruit, then it is a bad tree bearing bad fruit.

The defining marker of a bad tree is the fact that it cannot produce good fruit. We also know from Jesus' words that "religious" looking acts are not the markers of good fruit – "prophesying", "performing miracles", "driving out demons." Jesus calls them "evildoers." Such actions have the appearance of authenticity, but the lack true devotion to discipleship – the very thing that Jesus emphasizes or these showing displays. It is the holding to the teachings of Jesus that separates the sheep and the goats and Jesus knows very well those who are in the sheep pen.

Reflection and Practical Application

1. Read also Matthew 24:4-28 and Luke 17:23.
2. Think of some popular religious leaders and examine their message and life.
3. See which ones are bearing good fruit and which are not.

WEEK SIX

"Anyone who loves his father or mother more than me is not worthy of me; anyone who loves his son or daughter more than me is not worthy of me; and anyone who does not take his cross and follow me is not worthy of me. Whoever finds his life will lose it, and whoever loses his life for my sake will find it.

"He who receives you receives me, and he who receives me receives the one who sent me. Anyone who receives a prophet because he is a prophet will receive a prophet's reward, and anyone who receives a righteous man because he is a righteous man will receive a righteous man's reward. And if anyone gives even a cup of cold water to one of these little ones because he is my disciple, I tell you the truth, he will certainly not lose his reward." – **Matthew 10:37-42**

LOVE, TRUST AND OBEY

Day 26: Love, Trust and Obey

Love the Lord with all Your Heart

Our love for Jesus should baffle those around us. Many people hear a form of the gospel that excludes the words of Jesus refining our hearts. How can a man know what is truly in his heart unless it is tested? We know how much we love Jesus when our hearts are tested with these words. Do we love Jesus more than our father, mother, wife, son, daughter or even our own lives?

Trust in Jesus

"Do not let your hearts be troubled. Trust in God; trust also in me." – John 14:1

Put Faith in Jesus

"I tell you the truth, anyone who has faith in me will do what I have been doing. He will do even greater things than these, because I am going to the Father." – John 14:12

We love everything about Jesus accept how he chose to live. He made himself poor while making others rich. He often went without sleep, food or shelter. He was constantly focused on serving others and preaching the good news to the towns and villages around him. We love Jesus. We just simply do not love his life.

If we are to truly claim to have faith in Jesus, then we must live as he lived. If we are not living like Jesus, then we are not putting our faith in Jesus. We are putting our faith in money, jobs, savings, or investments. Jesus calls us to follow him in life and in love. It's lip service versus life service.

Obey Jesus

"If you love me, you will obey what I command." – John 14:15

"Whoever has my commands and obeys them, he is the one who loves me. He who loves me will be loved by my Father, and I too will love him and show myself to him." – John 14:21

In simple words, we know that if we claim to love Jesus we will obey what he commands. We trust and obey because we truly love. If we are not trusting or obeying, then we can be sure that our love is shallow and at best lip service to God. Jesus calls us to give up everything, trust him and follow him. How can we claim to love him if we don't trust him? And how can we claim to love him if we don't obey him?

Reflection and Practical Application

1. Determine what commands of Jesus you struggle to obey. Make a list of them.
2. Repent and begin obeying them as you put your trust in Jesus.
3. Pray to be strengthened in your faith so that you will continue to love and follow Jesus with your whole heart.

"Therefore keep watch, because you do not know on what day your Lord will come. But understand this: If the owner of the house had known at what time of night the thief was coming, he would have kept watch and would not have let his house be broken into. So you also must be ready, because the Son of Man will come at an hour when you do not expect him." – Matthew 24:42-44

KEEP WATCH

Day 27: Keep Watch

We are the owner's of our spiritual house. We have been put in charge by Jesus to guard the affairs of our household. Jesus tells us to "watch and pray" so that we will not fall into temptation. Satan comes at night to steal, kill and destroy and he waits for an opportune time when we have let our guard down. The worthless servant gets drunk and beats the other servants. Jesus warns us not to become like this servant, but to always be on our guard so that we can stand against Satan's schemes.

Read Matthew 25:1-30. Notice how in each parable Jesus has given us a certain responsibility that we must be faithful with until his return. The ten virgins were to keep their lamps burning and in order to do so they kept extra oil. The five foolish virgins did not do the work necessary in order to finish the race. The wise virgins did the work to maintain their godly journey and in the end they were found to have persevered. In the same way the workers who were given money to put to work were responsible for receiving back more than what they started with.

Keeping watch involves more than just remaining free from sin, we are to run the race marked out for us. There is a call and a mission that Jesus expects us to complete and only the wise servants will persevere to the end. These servants understood the mission and the cost. They prepared in advance to finish the assignment given to them by their master and in the end were rewarded.

Cut Off Sin

"Woe to the world because of the things that cause people to sin! Such things must come, but woe to the man through whom they come! If your hand or your foot causes you to sin, cut it off and throw it away. It is better for you to enter life maimed or crippled than to have two hands or two feet and be thrown into eternal fire. And if your eye causes you to sin, gouge it out and throw it away. It is better for you to enter life with one eye than to have two eyes and be thrown into the fire of hell." – Matthew 18:7-9

Equally important as being wise is being righteous. Our indignation toward sin should compare to the severity of the punishment Jesus had to suffer on the cross for our sin. The very nature of the cross shows how severe and devastating sin is to us.

Jesus wants us to paint a picture in our mind about the destructive nature of sin. Sin is like a cancer and if it infects one part of the body it will destroy the whole person. If we had cancer in our eye or hand, we would have it "cut off and thrown away." This is the stand Jesus wants us to take against sin. We must cut if off at every turn. Thankfully, our eyes, hands and feet do not cause us to sin, but our hearts do and we need to guard our hearts and be ever watchful to protect what Jesus has entrusted – the promised Holy Spirit.

Reflection and Practical Application

1. Pray today that God will help you avoid temptation.
2. Be open about your struggles and confess the ways in which you fall short and determine to always be open about temptation and sin particularly when you feel tempted to hide areas of your life you are embarrassed by.

WEEK FOUR

"Come to me, all you who are weary and burdened, and I will give you rest. Take my yoke upon you and learn from me, for I am gentle and humble in heart, and you will find rest for your souls. For my yoke is easy and my burden is light." – Matthew 11:28-30

LAY DOWN YOUR BURDENS

Day 28: Lay Down Your Burdens

Our Way vs. Jesus' Way

Jesus' way, easy. Our way, not so much. Even with such a radical call by Jesus to give up everything we have, Jesus confidently says his way and yoke is easy and his burden is light. Is it a burden to follow Jesus? Sure, following Jesus comes with its very own set of challenges and difficulties (For example – persecution). However, we have seen time and time again that those who pursue wealth and power are full of burdens and problems.

Jesus' burden (though still a burden) is easy and his yoke (though still a yoke) is light. The yoke of unbelief and greed is a heavy and difficult path, paved with hardship and heartache. When we are under this yoke, we are not under the control of a loving Savior, but a ruthless tyrant (Satan) who desires our complete destruction.

We face a daily temptation to take up our yokes again and pursue our own selfish gain, becoming once again burdened by Satan's schemes. Jesus calls us to take up our cross (His burden), deny ourselves and follow him (His yoke) on a daily basis.

Reflection and Practical Application

1. Have you ever had one of those days? Could it be that you've taken up your own burden again?
2. Decide today to deny yourself, continuing to do so daily, and take the yoke of Jesus in all your ways.
3. Think about your daily activity and pursuits and see if they are for the glory of God and the kingdom or your own agenda.
4. Make a list of the things that are fruitless branches.
5. Decide to lay these burdens down at the foot of the cross.

"The good man brings good things out of the good stored up in him, and the evil man brings evil things out of the evil stored up in him. But I tell you that men will have to give account on the day of judgment for every careless word they have spoken. For by your words you will be acquitted, and by your words you will be condemned."

– Matthew 12:35-37

CARELESS WORDS

Day 29: Careless Words

Good Storehouses

If our eyes are constantly fed darkness, then we will be filled with darkness. But if our eyes are filled with light (the Word), then we will be full of light (Matthew 6:22). In a very 'real' sense "we are what we eat." If our daily diet consists of the word of God and God's will, then we are storing up in ourselves the light of Christ. However, if our daily diet is full of evil things that flood our eyes and ears and hearts, then we are storing up in ourselves darkness. From the overflow of this darkness our mouths speak. It is this overflow that begins to identify who we are truly.

We have all been and have met those who seem to talk about everything but Christ. They have storehouses of useless information and become lost in spiritual conversations. Because we were all this way at one point we have the benefit of knowing what would have moved us from our dark place of empty words.

Reflection and Practical Application

1. Think of someone you know whose mouth is full of darkness (bitterness and cursing).
2. Think of what you were before you were called.
3. Think of ways in which the gospel could have penetrated your heart in that state.
4. Make a list of ways to reach this person or people.
5. Pray to God for guidance and wisdom.

"Be careful," **Jesus said to them.** "Be on your guard against the yeast of the Pharisees and Sadducees."

They discussed this among themselves and said, "It is because we didn't bring any bread."

Aware of their discussion, Jesus asked, "You of little faith, why are you talking among yourselves about having no bread? Do you still not understand? Don't you remember the five loaves for the five thousand, and how many basketfuls you gathered? Or the seven loaves for the four thousand, and how many basketfuls you gathered? How is it you don't understand that I was not talking to you about bread? But be on your guard against the yeast of the Pharisees and Sadducees." **Then they understood that he was not telling them to guard against the yeast used in bread, but against the teaching of the Pharisees and Sadducees."** – Matthew 16:6-12.

GUARD AGAINST HYPOCRISY

Day 30: Guard Against Hypocrisy

A Little Yeast

Jesus warns his disciples against hypocrisy in front of a crowd and uses the teachers of the Law and the Pharisees as prime examples. Read Matthew 23:1-38. Notice the indignation Jesus has toward the Pharisees and the Teachers of the Law. In our day these two names have become synonymous with "legalism" and "hypocrisy." Now imagine more current religious groups. What if Jesus said "Woe to you, _____?" What group do you think of that would fit in this blank? These are the people who pretend to be righteous yet their fruit smells rotten with selfishness and greed. These are the same people who love attention and lofty titles. They also love elaborate garments to be seen by men as important. Jesus is using these men as examples to us as what not to be like.

"Consider carefully what you hear," he continued. "With the measure you use, it will be measured to you—and even more." – Mark 4:24

What are our measurements, our standards or our expectations? Do we use Jesus' teachings as our standard or are we holding others to an unreasonable expectation because we highly favor our own sense of self-worth? The legalistic religious people of Jesus' day looked down on others who did not measure up to their standard. They neglected the robbed man (Luke 10:31-32). They took offense at the blind man (John 9:34). They wanted to stone the adulterous woman (John 8:5).

It is not surprising that Jesus described himself as a great physician (Mark 2:17). Jesus came for the sick, which seemed to be largely ignored by the Pharisees. What did the Pharisees do if they cared very little for the people who could have been greatly helped by them? Rather than help the weak, the Pharisees seemed more interested in destroying weak things and only strengthening strong things. In other words they cared more about themselves appearing like spiritual giants with little or no regard for the spiritually weak. Jesus says, "you experts in the law ... load people down with burdens they can hardly carry, and you yourselves will not lift a finger to help them" (Luke 11:46 NIV).

The student of Jesus only needs one title – "servant." Avoiding hypocrisy (which literally derives its meaning from acting on stage) is done by embracing the servant nature of Christ. Jesus says, "whoever would be great among you must be your servant, and whoever would be first must be slave of all" (Mark 10:43,44 ESV). What does Jesus want us to take away from this?

Reflection and Practical Application

1. Be unseen.
2. Refuse lofty titles: Master, Father, Teacher.
3. Consider carefully what you see and hear.

Part Four: GREATER HUMILITY

WEEK SEVEN

"I'm not interested in crowd approval. And do you know why? Because I know you and your crowds. I know that love, especially God's love, is not on your working agenda. I came with the authority of my Father, and you either dismiss me or avoid me. If another came, acting self-important, you would welcome him with open arms. How do you expect to get anywhere with God when you spend all your time jockeying for position with each other, ranking your rivals and ignoring God?" – **John 5:41-43 (MSG)**

PRAISE MAKE STUPID

Day 31: Praise Make Stupid

Do Not Accept Praise from Men

Jesus says he does not accept praise from men. How often is it that we look for praise for something we have said or done? Read John 5:41-43. It might appear at first notice that someone who is refusing praise is indeed humble. "What you did just now was spectacular!" "No, really it was nothing." "Nothing, you were wonderful. I can hardly contain my excitement you awesome person you." I've rather exaggerated slightly, but you get the scenario. Someone gives us high praise for something we did or said and we attempt to be humble by downplaying our abilities. I believe the truly humble person simply responds with a "Thank you." Whether it is conscience or not we elicit more praise by false humility than a genuine acknowledgement of the person's appreciation for our gifts.

Jesus sets the example by not only looking for praise, but refusing praise. We are not to confuse this praise with worship. Jesus is not saying he is refusing men's worship. However, Jesus adamantly refuses the praise from people that often is in the form of flattery. Most praise has attachments. When people praise others it is as if they are presenting the praise as a favor or payment with an expectation of something in return. Why do people shower certain people with flattering words of praise and platitudes? It is evident we do not see this outpouring of praise equally with everyone. Is it to curry favor or to gain recognition for ourselves through association?

Worship is not this way. When we worship we are expecting nothing. We are bowing in obeisance to God showing how much he has given us – it is we who owe and we offer that in praise. However flattery has the effect of making us stupid. Flattery is the opposite of righteous correction.

"Whoever loves discipline loves knowledge, but whoever hates correction is stupid." – Proverbs 12:1 (NIV)

The person who loves flattery hates correction. They can never admit to being wrong and will take great offense at anyone who holds an opposing view.

"For such (divisive) people are not serving our Lord Christ, but their own appetites. By smooth talk and flattery they deceive the minds of naïve people" (Romans 16:18 NIV). Naïve people aren't typically considered the brightest bulbs in the bunch. Smooth talk and flattery can only deceive the kind of people who love them both. Flattery reduces a person's intellectual capacity and makes them less discerning. They lose their ability to be wise in matters of importance. This is why the Proverb says, "A flattering tongue works ruin" (Proverbs 26:28 NIV).

Reflection and Practical Application

1. In what areas do you need to guard your heart against flattery?
2. How has flattery blinded you toward some important matters that you have neglected?
3. Focus on ways to acknowledge others' appreciation without falling victim to praise.

"Stop judging by mere appearances and make a right judgment." – **John 7:24**

A FOOL IS ALWAYS RIGHT

Day 32: A Fool is Always Right

Make Right Judgments

Judging by outward appearances places us in the category of fools. A fool is always right by making glib judgments. Jesus appeared to the world in the form of a helpless child. Outwardly, Jesus appears helpless and poor. Through divine revelation we know this child was sent to be the savior of the world. It is not a coincidence that wise men understood the times and the significance of this infant.

The Pharisees judged Jesus by mere outward appearance and disparaged anyone believing that this man from Galilee could be the

Messiah. As humans we are tempted to make judgments based on what we see. We formerly judged Jesus in this way. To us he was poor and without significance. Paul says, "we once regarded Christ [from a worldly point of view]" (2 Corinthians 5:16 NIV).

Interestingly, it was what the Pharisees thought they understood from Scriptures that caused them to say such harsh things to anyone who acknowledge that Jesus could possibly be the Christ. The Pharisees make the claim that no prominent (rulers) people or Pharisees believe Jesus of Nazareth could be the Christ. "Large crowds only follow Jesus because they don't know anything about the law – a cursed bunch of idiots" (John 7:47-49 paraphrased).

Now to the truly wise, Jesus is Lord of all and ruler of his kingdom. We once judged one another in this way. We based friendships on class, race and sex. We were judging by mere outward appearances. Looking past the flesh is difficult and does not come easily. Proverbs 20:5 says, "The purposes of a man's heart is like deep water, but a man of understanding will draw it out" (ESV). So many layers exist behind the surface of a person, but "right" judgment – that is a judgment of understanding and wisdom can see beyond the surface and peer deep into the waters of someone's heart.

The heart of God existed all the time in Jesus even when he was perceived to be a glutton and a drunkard, but only the pure in heart could see God in the flesh. How much of God's presence do we miss when we make wrong judgments?

We are no longer subject to worldly perspectives and judgments. In Christ we are all one and we are called not to judge as we did in the world. It will take us out of our comfort zone. It will cause us to make spiritually discerning judgments rather than surface and quick judgments.

All these warnings have the goal of keeping us from being hypocrites. If we guard our hearts against these things we will do well in avoiding the yeast of the Pharisees and make "right judgments."

Reflection and Practical Application

1. What have been some quick judgments you have made about others in the past?
2. Have you been on the receiving end of someone else's judgment of you?
3. Do you expect to be judged critically when you are overly critical of others?
4. Has the poor treatment from others caused you to view judging in your heart differently?

WEEK FIVE

"I tell you the truth, unless you change and become like little children, you will never enter the kingdom of heaven. Therefore, whoever humbles himself like this child is the greatest in the kingdom of heaven.

And whoever welcomes a little child like this in my name welcomes me. But if anyone causes one of these little ones who believe in me to sin, it would be better for him to have a large millstone hung around his neck and to be drowned in the depths of the sea."

– Matthew 18:3-6 (NIV)

THE GREATEST IN THE KINGDOM

Day 33: The Greatest in the Kingdom

Humble Yourself

Humility is that quality that most believe they can always improve on. However, humility is a command and not a virtue that we will naturally have. Our natural selves desire to be first, to be seen, and to be recognized. Humility desires to put others first and considers others better than themselves. Humility is a choice. We can choose to put ourselves first or others. We can choose to be unseen or take glory and praise for ourselves. We can choose to be humble or we can choose pride and arrogance.

"Sitting down, Jesus called the Twelve and said, "If anyone wants to be first, he must be the very last, and the servant of all." – **Mark 9:35**

The arrogant often desire to be served and look at leadership as a position where others exists for their benefit. However, in Christ this is not so. We who are called to lead must serve and we who are to be first must be a slave to all. When we think of the humility of a slave, we begin to picture the type of character Jesus desires us to show toward one another.

Reflection and Practical Application

1. Read Luke 14:8-11. What does this passage say about humility?
2. Think of a situation that you may encounter this week that you can decide to take a position of humility.
3. Ask your discipler how your humility is perceived by others.
4. Imagine others as your master and how you would respond to an earthly master.

"A new command I give you: Love one another. As I have loved you, so you must love one another. By this all men will know that you are my disciples, if you love one another." **– John 13:34, 35.**

LOVE ONE ANOTHER LIKE JESUS

Day 34: Love One Another Like Jesus

A New Command

Loving like Jesus takes a willingness to lower our own high sense of self-importance. This does not mean we lower our sense of self-worth because God treats us as his priceless treasure. However, we think highly of ourselves above others, whom God also values with great esteem.

Jesus calls us to love one another. We know this command. We can quote this command. We tell others this command because of how it identifies true disciples. However, the most significant part of

Jesus' words found in John 13:34 is the very fact that ***it is a command***. It is not for us to do as we feel motivated to do. It is not to do as long as we like those around us or as others continue to like us or not wrong us. We are to obey this command – it is a command of Jesus. It is significant and important enough that Jesus conveys it as a command. He does not imply it by a story or parable or even in actions alone. Jesus is very explicit and tells us directly that this is what we are to do regardless of our emotions, moods or if we are feeling great spiritually.

Jesus is letting us know that at the core of a disciple is love and if we are going to reproduce disciples, then we are going to reproduce the love that Jesus demonstrated. Jesus' command to love one another avoids ambiguity because he tells us to love as he has loved us. Jesus even demonstrates his love by washing the feet of the disciples. Are we above washing someone else's feet?

Reflection and Practical Application

1. Have you ever washed the feet of another disciple?
2. Have you ever thought Jesus' words were too literal to apply to today's cultural setting?
3. Would you refuse to let someone wash your feet? Peter did, but Jesus washed his feet anyway.
4. Would you refuse to let Jesus wash your feet?

"Now that I, your Lord and Teacher, have washed your feet, you also should wash one another's feet." **– John 13:14.**

THE AGONY OF THE FEET

Day 35: The Agony of the Feet

Wash the Feet of One Another (Literally)

Regardless of how we wish to interpret this passage we are to obey Jesus' words. We can justify how in that day they wore sandals and walked in dirt all day so it was customary to wash a person's feet as they entered a home. Well, it could just be me, but my feet still endure some abuse throughout the day and they are fairly stinky and in need of some love. Even if we only apply the spiritual applications of this command, we still find many falling short of this command. We wash each other's feet because it is a kindness. Are we not able to wash our own feet? The last I checked I could reach my toes. I'm sure Jesus disciples could reach their own toes as well. Are we somehow better equipped to wash our feet easier than the disciples in the first-century? It is not for that reason that Jesus calls us to wash the feet of one another. We wash each other's feet because it is humility. Would the President of the United States come and wash your feet? Probably not, unless of course he is a disciple. So we see it is this act of love that bears the mark of humility that is significant.

Reflection and Practical Application

1. Could there be a direct link between our level of humility and our willingness to wash someone else's feet?
2. Think of someone whose feet you can wash. Then actually wash their feet.
3. Think of something to do that is truly loving toward your brothers and sisters. Your act should go beyond a friendly greeting at service. Does anyone need help spiritually or physically? How eager are you to serve the needs of your spiritual family when it comes to cleaning, feeding, visiting or assisting?

WEEK EIGHT

"If your brother sins against you, go and show him his fault, just between the two of you. If he listens to you, you have won your brother over. But if he will not listen, take one or two others along, so that 'every matter may be established by the testimony of two or three witnesses.' If he refuses to listen to them, tell it to the church; and if he refuses to listen even to the church, treat him as you would a pagan or a tax collector.

I tell you the truth, whatever you bind on earth will be bound in heaven, and whatever you loose on earth will be loosed in heaven.

Again, I tell you that if two of you on earth agree about anything you ask for, it will be done for you by my Father in heaven. For where two or three come together in my name, there am I with them."

— Matthew 18:15-20

HELP FOR THE HURT

Day 36: Help for the Hurt

Win Your Brother Over

Why would Jesus have the offended party seek restitution? If we think about it for a moment it only makes sense. If our brother sins against us, he is not thinking spiritually to say, "Wow. I really should not have sinned against that person that way. Let me go ask for forgiveness." Or he may be completely oblivious to the fact that he sinned.

Either way Jesus puts the ball square in our court and has us going to get the matter resolved. This is also an urgent matter we should address. We should not let the sun go down before we do. Why? Well, I can see Matthew 18 reading, "While you are still spiritual, go and show him his fault." Because what typically happens when someone offends us? We become angry and in our anger we sin. The temptation is to go from hurt, to offended, to retaliation. In the retaliation stage we can either be overt in our attack or subtle by holding a grudge. Jesus helps us avoid these stages by dealing with the matter quickly.

We are even given alternate ways of resolving the issue if our first efforts go unnoticed. There are few things more damaging than expressing genuine hurt to someone who does not listen to you. If we were left with only option one, we may find ourselves in a scenario that causes even more hurt to the offended person.

"You hurt my feelings and I believe you sinned against me with your unkind words. Being unkind is not godly and it is hurtful."

"I wasn't trying to be mean, that's just who I am. You really need to toughen up a bit and grow thicker skin."

Clearly, the person has not listened or been won over. So what are we to do next? Jesus tells us to grab another brother or sister (preferably someone who witnessed the situation, though not expressly stated) and bring them with us to have one more sit down heart to heart talk.

This is now the second time we are confronting this person about their sinful actions. Surely, they will listen this time. Not exactly.

"I'm not sure why you brought Brother 'So-and-so' with you, but both of you need to get over this and move on!"

Seriously? Well, we have another option we are given by Jesus for such a response. We are free at this point to let the church know. This is not gossip and should be done in a formal way (although not expressly stated). This is a way for the offending person to develop a conviction about their sinful behavior. Currently, they are flattering themselves too much to detect their sin. However, with the weight of the entire church acknowledging that this behavior is spiritually unacceptable, they have a greater opportunity to repent.

If a person is still unable to see their fault after each of these steps are applied in the grace and heart they are intended by Jesus (to win them over), then we are simply called to treat them as we would a pagan or a tax collector. This too can be a bit tricky because it simply means we no longer hold this person to the standard of discipleship – in the same way we would not hold a Pagan to the standard of Jesus.

Jesus does not command these things to give us a way to retaliate by treating someone harshly (i.e., our perceived way of treating a pagan or tax collector). If we give it more careful thought we realize how we are called to treat our "enemies" – with love. At this point all we can do is love the brother or sister and release them from the expectation that they will respond in a godly manner.

"And the Lord's servant must not be quarrelsome but kind to everyone, able to teach, patiently enduring evil, correcting his opponents with gentleness. God may perhaps grant them repentance leading to a knowledge of the truth, and they may come to their senses and escape from the snare of the devil, after being captured by him to do his will." (2 Timothy 2:24-26 ESV).

We must understand that our fight is not against flesh and blood but against Satan's schemes. Satan captures people to be a snare to you so that you will stumble and be tempted to retaliate and hold anger and hatred in your heart because someone wrongs you. You are called to endure evil and patiently go through the process of guarding your heart and winning your brother or sister over with grace and forgiveness. This is Jesus' way.

Reflection and Practical Application

1. What people or person is in your life that you have yet to confront biblically?
2. Are you more afraid of not being heard or coming off like a crazy person with emotional issues?
3. How can prayer and meditating on God's word improve your ability to hold to Matthew 18:15?

"Do not judge, or you too will be judged. For in the same way you judge others, you will be judged, and with the measure you use, it will be measured to you.

"Why do you look at the speck of sawdust in your brother's eye and pay no attention to the plank in your own eye? How can you say to your brother, 'Let me take the speck out of your eye,' when all the time there is a plank in your own eye? You hypocrite, first take the plank out of your own eye, and then you will see clearly to remove the speck from your brother's eye." – Matthew 7:1-5

PLANK vs. SPECK

Day 37: Plank vs. Speck

Remove the Plank

What a great temptation it is to be judgmental when our brother or sister sin against us. Since we don't sin against anyone in this way (or so we think), then we find it hard to understand why someone would sin against us in this way. "Why does brother such and such wrong me like this?" Or, "Why does sister 'so and so' keep sinning against me in this way." We might think our situation is different because the people we deal with are unrepentant. They constantly keep doing the same things. Well, unrepentant and continuing to do the same things are actually two different things. If we address someone's sin and they listen and then immediately turn around and do the same thing in the same day, then we are called to forgive. However, if they refuse to listen when we do address the sin, then this is being unrepentant and we have a response that is given to us by Jesus for this situation.

Reflection and Practical Application

1. Decide to resolve matters quickly.
2. Maintain the heart of winning over your brother or sister rather than seeking justice for a hurt or wrong.

"Then Peter came to Jesus and asked, "Lord, how many times shall I forgive my brother when he sins against me? Up to seven times?"

Jesus answered, "I tell you, not seven times, but seventy-seven times."
– Matthew 18:21-22

BE A WELL OF FORGIVENESS

Day 38: Be a Well of Forgiveness

77 Times

Most of us would not consider ourselves unmerciful. However, this is exactly what Jesus calls us when we fail to forgive. Jesus died on the cross for our sins and our sins outweigh any amount we could pay. Our debt to God is beyond repayment which has been freely paid by Christ. When we look at others as having more need of forgiveness or in some way having sinned worse than us, then we have lost touch with our own debt and we have become ungrateful for the gift given us.

The Parable of the Unmerciful Servant

"Therefore, the kingdom of heaven is like a king who wanted to settle accounts with his servants. As he began the settlement, a man who owed him ten thousand talents was brought to him. Since he was not able to pay, the master ordered that he and his wife and his children and all that he had be sold to repay the debt.

"The servant fell on his knees before him. 'Be patient with me,' he begged, 'and I will pay back everything.' The servant's master took pity on him, canceled the debt and let him go.

"But when that servant went out, he found one of his fellow servants who owed him a hundred denarii. He grabbed him and began to choke him. 'Pay back what you owe me!' he demanded.

"His fellow servant fell to his knees and begged him, 'Be patient with me, and I will pay you back.'

"But he refused. Instead, he went off and had the man thrown into prison until he could pay the debt. When the other servants saw what had happened, they were greatly distressed and went and told their master everything that had happened.

"Then the master called the servant in. 'You wicked servant,' he said, 'I canceled all that debt of yours because you begged me to. Shouldn't you have had mercy on your fellow servant just as I had on you?' In anger his master turned him over to the jailers to be tortured, until he should pay back all he owed.

"This is how my heavenly Father will treat each of you unless you forgive your brother from your heart." – Matthew 18:23-35

Losing gratitude happens on an almost daily basis. When we receive something new or a wonderful gift we have joy that day and it diminishes the very next day. It diminishes even faster when we fail to praise God for what we received. Each day we try harder to muster praise for what we have and then eventually we forget to mention it at all. When we lose gratitude we become judgmental and our own forgiveness for others diminishes.

Reflection and Practical Application

1. How often do we thank God for our health when we are well?
2. What about our jobs, homes, clothes, family?
3. Have we forgotten already to rejoice and thank God for our gift of forgiveness?

"I am the true vine." – **John 15:1 (NIV)**

REMAIN IN ME

Day 39: Remain in Me

Jesus says his command is to love each other. How do we remain in Jesus? Read John 15:1-17. We must continue in love. Love is the universal adhesive that bonds us together despite our differences.

Love is the agent of change that persists and forces its way through the impenetrable barriers of pride and resistance. Love is the catalyst that ignites a people to organize and accomplish great things in the name of Jesus. Love settles issues that threaten the fabric of unity and fosters peace. We need love more than any plan of action. Without love we become liars and the truth does not live in us or the knowledge of God.

Be United

"Sanctify them in the truth; your word is truth. As you sent me into the world, so I have sent them into the world. And for their sake I consecrate myself, that they also may be sanctified in truth.

"I do not ask for these only, but also for those who will believe in me through their word, that they may all be one, just as you, Father, are in me, and I in you, that they also may be in us, so that the world may believe that you have sent me. The glory that you have given me I have given to them, that they may be one even as we are one, I in them and you in me, that they may become perfectly one, so that the world may know that you sent me and loved them even as you loved me. Father, I desire that they also, whom you have given me, may be with me where I am, to see my glory that you have given me because you loved me before the foundation of the world." John 17:17-24

How important is unity to you personally? We don't think of unity much in our daily lives unless we are faced with a situation that calls us to fight for the survival of unity within a group or organization. When we are separate, we are defeated.

It took several years before I could see Satan's scheme to destroy the church through disunity. Never before had I associated destruction with disunity until I imagined by own body in complete disunity. If my hands and arms were separate, my legs and feet, my upper body from my lower body and my head from my neck were all separate then anyone on the outside looking at my body would conclude that I had been destroyed. It doesn't take an active imagination to visualize the crime scene of a person in this condition. Yet we do not see the body of Christ this way.

Remaining in Jesus Christ is having the same heart toward unity as he did. How have you worked to increase the unity around you? Does pride and arrogance cause you to separate yourself from others? Do you notice these characteristics in others yet refuse to address them for the sake of your brother or sister, but more importantly for the good of the body of Christ?

Do Not Disassociate or Discriminate

Read Acts 10:9-15. Are your friendships comfortable? Do you only associate with people who are like you or look like you? Jesus desires that his house be full and full of all people from all nations.

Remember the "Least" Brothers

Read Matthew 25:31-40. Who is "least" among you in your fellowship? Have you visited them? Have you assisted them? Have you met their needs or made your friendship known to them?

Reflection and Practical Application

1. Meditate on these passages.
2. Decide to become more active in the lives of your "lesser" brothers and sisters.

"While they were eating, Jesus took bread, gave thanks and broke it, and gave it to his disciples, saying, "Take and eat; this is my body."

Then he took the cup, gave thanks and offered it to them, saying, "Drink from it, all of you. This is my blood of the covenant, which is poured out for many for the forgiveness of sins." – **Matthew 26:26-28**

DO THIS

Day 40: Do This

There is only one gospel writer who includes the command to remember Jesus through communion. Luke writes, "do this in remembrance of me." Ironically, the gospel writers and authors who actually pass this teaching on in writings were not physically present during the Lord's Supper. John and Matthew were both present during the Lord's Supper, but do not include this particular command in their gospel accounts. John gives us that great command in John 13:34. John's account focused more on what happened during this last meal and the newest command Jesus gives on loving each other.

Remember Me

"And he said to them, "I have eagerly desired to eat this Passover with you before I suffer. For I tell you, I will not eat it again until it finds fulfillment in the kingdom of God."

"After taking the cup, he gave thanks and said, "**Take this and divide it among you.** For I tell you I will not drink again of the fruit of the vine until the kingdom of God comes."

And he took bread, gave thanks and broke it, and gave it to them, saying, "This is my body given for you; do this in remembrance of me."

In the same way, after the supper he took the cup, saying, "This cup is the new covenant in my blood, which is poured out for you." – **Luke 22:15-20**

Omitting Jesus' words does not take away from its significance. **There are some passages that fail to mention repentance or baptism** or even belief, but it is understood that the audience is already familiar with these concepts and to mention them would be repetitive or cloud the emphasis of the passage. Additionally, we are in no way short of making traditions out of "mole hills." **Celebrating communion is a well known tradition** and even Paul's mention of it to the church in Corinth was to correct the behavior of those participating and not necessarily reminding them to actually take communion. Also noteworthy, is the confusion of communion with the Passover meal. Although there were people getting drunk and gorging themselves, communion was not a meal. As noted in the

Passover feast, Jesus and his disciples ate the Passover meal, but communion was in addition to the meal. In the same way the disciples in Corinth had a meal as they had communion. This is the most likely reason Paul referenced them having homes to eat in.

There is no mention by any authors the frequency to which we take, participate or have communion. Some celebrate communion once a month. Others once a year and still many once a week. Paul implies once a week because this is also his direction on the money collected for God's people. However, Paul only mentions "when you come together." This implies each time we come together as a body, which can still be interpreted as the first day of the week since we know we at least meet that day to make the collection for God's people.

However, we know based on the book of Acts that the disciples met every day. It is most likely that Paul's direction was implying that as often as we meet (whether once a week or more often) that we celebrate communion and remember Jesus. Additionally the first day of the week is when Jesus rose from the dead. There are two perspectives that can come from this notion. The first is this is a possible fulfillment of Jesus' words, "I will not drink again of the fruit of the vine until the kingdom of God comes." It could be interpreted that after Jesus raised from the dead that he took communion, thereby moving it from Friday (the night he was betrayed) to Sunday (the day he rose). There is no written account of Jesus drinking of the cup on the day of his resurrection. However, we know Jesus broke bread with his disciples on the day of his resurrection. Luke mentions this in chapter 24 verse 30, "When he was at the table with them, he took bread, gave thanks, broke it and began to give it to them." Jesus also eats with Peter as they have breakfast the next morning. However, this is an unlikely reason as Joseph is still waiting for the kingdom to arrive after Jesus' resurrection.

The most likely intent of Jesus' words and Paul's conveyance of Jesus' words would be simply to **remember**. Regardless of what day of the week we remember, whether Friday, Sunday, or whatever day, we are called to remember. As often as we come together we are to remember. Some object to children taking communion, but I find no objection in Scripture and can even imagine Jesus rebuking us for such a practice. If a child knows what to remember, Jesus commands us not to hinder them.

Reflection and Practical Application

1. When you come together as a local body – have communion.
2. Take communion in a worthy manner – recognize Christ.
3. When you receive the cups that have been divided (note Luke 22:17) wait for each other.
4. Think of ways to facilitate communion. Volunteer to help or bake communion bread.

"Then Jesus came to them and said, "All authority in heaven and on earth has been given to me. Therefore go and make disciples of all nations, baptizing them in the name of the Father and of the Son and of the Holy Spirit, and teaching them to obey everything I have commanded you. And surely I am with you always, to the very end of the age." **– Matthew 28:18-20**

GO MAKE DISCIPLES

Day 41: Go Make Disciples

Today is the last study in our series and marks the 41st day of walking in the ways of Jesus. Several great works have been written that encompass 40 days of deep devotional study. However, it was not the 40th day that Jesus began his ministry, but on the 41st day – the day after he emerged from the desert. Rather than a desert, we have learned at the foot of Jesus' words, reclining at his table of wisdom. Prayerfully, this has been a journey that has brought you closer to walking with Jesus. Hopefully, you will continue to imitate those who model Jesus around you and be motivated to grow in your discipleship as you eat from the Master's table.

Go and Make Disciples

The significance of Jesus' words are sometimes missed and often overlooked as being the critical part of his command. Jesus tells us to "Go" which requires us to actually move from our position. As great as a fisherman might be, the fish will not just climb out of the water and place themselves cleaned and cooked on our plate. We have to go and find water. And then find water that is teeming with fish.

Jesus also says, "make." Some people shy away from the word "make" when it comes to preaching the gospel. We might say things like, "I can't make you do anything." This is not true and our very use of the word "make" in other contexts proves that. For example, if I see a friend who is sad, I may say to them, "I'm going to make you feel better." I don't say, "I can't make you feel better because I can't make you do anything." No. On the contrary the latter statement would seem harsh and cruel. Such is the same when we say we can't make people do anything as we refrain from preaching the whole truth of the gospel.

We are called to "make" them into disciples. This also requires some forethought. If I am going to cheer someone up, then I need an idea of what I will do in order to accomplish that. Fortunately, Jesus gives us the tools we need as we all have been gifted with the Holy Spirit and his word. However, we must put our faith into action by actually putting a plan behind it.

Nothing else matters if we fail to do the most significant step, which is to make a "disciple." If we set out without a plan to make disciples, we are setting out to make anything but disciples. We are not called to make "good people," or "church members" or even leaders. We are called to go and make disciples. If we cannot answer the question as to how we make disciples, then ultimately we are not making disciples. If we cannot teach someone else what to do to make disciples, then most likely, we are not making disciples.

Go and Bear Fruit

Read John 15:1-17. What is Jesus asking us to do? Just as we are to go and make disciples we are to go and bear fruit – fruit that will last. Read also Matthew 13:1-23. Jesus says the "seed" is the "message about the kingdom" and anyone with good soil will produce more of the same – bearing fruit yielding a hundred, sixty, or thirty times what was sown. What was sown? The message about the kingdom was sown.

This is why Jesus says the Father will prune and make us more fruitful or cut off what does not produce fruit. Does God cut us off for not preaching the message of the kingdom? Insight to this can be found in 2 Corinthians 4:13, "I believed; therefore I have spoken." The Holy Spirit also supports this in Romans 11:11-21 and Hebrews 3:19. "We stand by faith" and it is by our belief that we speak. If we have no faith, we have no message and we are "broken off because of unbelief." Therefore, we are not cut off because we fail to preach, but because we fail to *believe* and love.

Share Your Faith with Family

"As Jesus was getting into the boat, the man who had been demon-possessed begged to go with him. Jesus did not let him, but said, "Go home to your family and tell them how much the Lord has done for you, and how he has had mercy on you." – Mark 5:18-19

Pearls to Pigs

"Do not give dogs what is sacred; do not throw your pearls to pigs. If you do, they may trample them under their feet, and then turn and tear you to pieces." – **Matthew 7:6**

Jesus' command to treat what is sacred with special treatment can sometimes be difficult to understand and obey. On the one hand we are compelled to preach the gospel to everyone under the sun – to all creatures. Then on the other hand we are to discriminate who we preach the gospel to. Does this mean we fill our churches with one type of people? Absolutely not. However, there are those who only consume time with arguments and resistant minds. There are too many open people in the harvest field to throw the pearls of the gospel to stupid arguments that produce nothing.

Remember the Story of Mary in the Cross Study

Read Matthew 26:6-13. Jesus is anointed with perfume before he goes to the cross. Jesus tells his disciples that this act will be told in memory of her wherever the gospel is preached. An indirect command to include Mary's story in the gospel (This is Mary the sister of Lazarus).

Don't Fear, Keep Preaching

Read Acts 18:9. Jesus encourages Paul to keep preaching. We know a silent Christian endures no persecution. The gospel is what brings persecution and we see its power by how much Satan wants to silence those who preach it. We must not be afraid or give in to fear. We have to continue preaching.

Unworthy Servant

"So you also, when you have done everything you were told to do, should say, 'We are unworthy servants; we have only done our duty.'"
– Luke 17:10

At the end of the day we are only doing what we were told to do. Jesus gives us these commands and by obeying them does not make us somehow more special than others. It makes us unworthy servants who did the job we were given. We are unworthy to have been given such a task and responsibility. Our calling is far beyond our qualifications. We should all be in the spiritual "mailroom," but Jesus has made us partners with him.

Follow Me!

Read John 21:15-22. Jesus reinstates Peter and narrows his attention as to the calling he has received. Peter deflects Jesus' words until Jesus tells Peter to simply "follow." We are often concerned about a great deal of other matters, but what it all boils down to is following Jesus. Walking as disciples, making disciples, worshiping God, loving, giving, praying – in all that we are and do we are following Jesus. This is Jesus' command – to follow him, even to death.

Reflection and Practical Application

1. Commit yourself wholeheartedly to the work of the Lord.
2. Multiply your talents by using them to win souls for Christ.
3. Learn to be more effective in evangelism by "putting your talents on deposit" with another disciple – that is pairing with someone who can show you how to be more effective.

Divide and Multiply
How Small Groups Make Big Churches

Ace McClinton

You are either a church of small groups or you are a church with small groups. The latter tend to miss the powerful building blocks of small group ministries. These key "signature ministries" are the catalytic agents that forcefully advance the kingdom of God in a time when churches that have a biblical kingdom model are desperately needed.

Divide and Multiply is the second book in the Growing Faith series and will challenge church leaders that desire to grow their local ministries to begin thinking both small and large simultaneously. Rather than focus on achieving the next milestone of the next one-hundred members, *Divide and Multiply* challenges the traditional thinking of the local pastor to become a global evangelist by first investing in small groups of missionary-minded men and women.

Available Soon in Stores and Online!

ALELETOS.COM

Where Do We Grow From Here?
Getting Unstuck

Ace McClinton

Many church leaders find their ministries reaching a plateau that appear to be inescapable. Unfortunately, church leaders who find themselves unable to solve the critical problems facing their ministries begin the inevitable road toward a declining ministry.

Churches are living, breathing organisms and as such have a life-cycle. Church leaders that do not plan and act within these life-cycles find their ministries stuck in a loop of unproductive work that leads to burned out leaders and disheartened members.

Where Do We Grow From Here? is the final book in the Growing Faith series. This book intends to provide the answers that tackle church growth issues and more while giving church leaders the tools they need to find the necessary momentum to produce break-out churches – finally getting their ministry unstuck!

Available Soon in Stores and Online!

Additional Resources

Help support

Aleletos Publishing Media Ministries

#GrowingFaithSeries

www.ingramcontent.com/pod-product-compliance
Lightning Source LLC
LaVergne TN
LVHW011417080426
835512LV00005B/118